The Best
of
Dear
Abby

The Best of Dear Abby

Abigail Van Buren

Andrews and McMeel, Inc.
A Universal Press Syndicate Company
Kansas City • New York • Washington

Library of Congress Cataloging in Publication Data

Van Buren, Abigail, 1918-
   The Best of Dear Abby.

   1. Conduct of life. I. Title. II. Title: Dear Abby.
BJ1581.2.V34   158   81-12821
ISBN 0-8362-7907-7   AACR2

for Mort

Contents

1

Dear Readers

Exactly twenty-five years ago, I, Pauline Esther Phillips, conceived and gave birth to Abigail Van Buren—better known as Dear Abby.

But let's start at the beginning:

When I came into the world on July 4, 1918, in Sioux City, Iowa, I was named Pauline Esther Friedman. My identical twin sister, who had made her debut just seventeen minutes earlier, had been named Esther Pauline. From that day on we were known as "the Friedman Twins."

As soon as we were old enough to talk, my twin called me "Popo" and I called her "Eppie." Friends who knew us B.C. (Before Column) still use those names, although the world has since come to know us as "Dear Abby" and "Ann Landers."

From my earliest recollections we were a team. We looked alike, talked alike, thought alike, and Mama always dressed us alike. We were precocious, mischievous, talkative, extroverted and cute. We were also creative. As children we were constantly collaborating on poems, parodies, and witty letters.

The Friedman Twins were always the center of attention. We worked up a little song-and-dance routine which we would deliver at the drop of a suggestion. We memorized nearly every song the Andrews Sisters had recorded and meticulously imitated their style and arrangements. And as if that weren't enough, we also played the violin!

Although we weren't particularly talented, whenever we performed we stopped the show. Not because we were good, but for amateurs we were incredibly confident, uninhibited, eager to please, and—to top it off—we were identical.

When we were in our early teens, our father bought an interest in a small circuit of theaters. One featured vaudeville, but Daddy never wanted "his twins" to be in show business. He had hoped that one day we would become lawyers—his own unfulfilled ambition. But having come to America as a poor immigrant from Russia with a bride to support, Abraham Friedman found education a luxury he could not afford.

Eppie and I were good students. Not great, but good enough to consistently bring home the kind of report cards that made our parents proud of us. And because parental approval had always been high on our list of priorities, we carefully avoided the more difficult subjects lest they mar our fine scholastic record.

Although we never qualified as genuine intellectuals, we had a way of attracting intellectuals, disarming them, and learning from them.

During our high school and college years the Friedman Twins were known as the life of the party—never at a loss for words. If one of us couldn't come up with a witty rejoinder or a snappy comeback, the other one could.

We were not only good talkers, we were good listeners. We always had more boyfriends than girlfriends. But that didn't bother us. We had each other.

Although we grew up during the Depression, our home was rich with love. We never heard our mother call our father Abraham. And he never addressed her as Rebecca. It was always Darling, Sweetheart, or Dear.

Discipline? You bet! Our parents were the government and we were the people. No debates and no backtalk. Their authority was never questioned.

Mama led us to believe that Papa was the boss, but in reality, Mama ran the family. Together they presented a united front. If they ever disagreed, it wasn't in front of their children.

We twins were the youngest of four daughters and the only two who pursued professional careers.

After graduating from high school my twin sister and I enrolled at Morningside, the local college. We had dreams of going to Northwestern University but were told we couldn't afford it. That may have been true, but our two older sisters had married and left home, and I suspect our parents wanted to keep their youngest around as long as possible.

Because we enjoyed writing, we signed up for the journalism course in our freshman year. We immediately started writing for the college weekly, and together we originated a lively little gossip column which we named "The Campus Rat."

We also took courses in philosophy, biology, English literature, and theology, but the only degrees we hold today are honorary, because we dropped out during our junior year to marry.

On July 2, 1939 (just two days before their twenty-first birthday), the Friedman Twins co-starred in a spectacular double-feature wedding. It was a production the likes of which Sioux City had never seen before—or since.

There was standing-room only in the flower-filled synagogue where friends and relatives had come to see a very proud father walk down the aisle with a twin bride on each arm.

I married Morton Phillips, a precocious student at the University of Minnesota, who lacked a month of being twenty-one.

The early years of our marriage were spent in Eau Claire, Wisconsin, where Mort ran the family-owned Presto Cooker Company. Eppie and her husband soon moved to Eau Claire when her husband, Jules Lederer, joined the Presto team.

Eppie and I soon became Eau Claire's most energetic volunteers. Name the cause—one of us headed it. Mental Health, Gray Ladies, United Crusade, the Easter Seal Society, B'nai Brith Women's Auxiliary, and the Democratic Party.

Incidentally, somewhere between all this volunteering, during the first five years of my marriage I volunteered for motherhood twice and was rewarded with a daughter, Jeanne, and a son, Edward, both now in their thirties and married. (Thank God!) To Edward and his wife I am indebted for having made me a grandmother twice.

In 1955 Mort bought a business in San Francisco and we headed for California. When we moved west, Eppie and her husband moved to Chicago.

After we were settled in our suburban Hillsborough home, I took stock of myself. I was a thirty-seven-year-old housewife with two teen-agers, plenty of help in the house, and time on my hands. I was bursting with energy.

I promptly volunteered my services to the San Mateo County Mental Health Association, the Easter Seal Society, the P.T.A., and the Temple Sisterhood.

Then Eppie, herself a newcomer to Chicago, phoned with some exciting news. A friend of hers who was an executive with the *Chicago Sun-Times* newspaper syndicate had called to tell her that Ruth Crowley, the woman who had been writing the syndicate-owned Ann Landers column, had died suddenly and they needed a replacement. Was Eppie interested in competing for the job?

Was she ever! (At that time, the Ann Landers column had a comparatively modest syndication, which has increased impressively since Eppie took over.)

For the first few months Eppie sent me batches of letters from readers, and I'd shoot back my suggested replies. Many were used, and I became fascinated with the opportunity to do something creative, entertaining, and helpful. I was ecstatically happy and having a ball!

Then, suddenly, the ball was over. Eppie called to say that her syndicate had put the kibosh on her sending mail "outside the office," so there would be no more letters coming my way.

Having acquired a taste for dispensing advice, and confident that I could do it well, I pondered the possibilities of writing an advice column locally.

I first called on the *San Mateo Times,* a small daily newspaper located about ten minutes from my home. I asked to see the feature editor, whose name I have now forgotten, but (if he's still alive) I'm sure he hasn't forgotten mine.

After cooling my heels outside his office for half an hour, I was ushered in.

I wasted no words in telling him that I thought his newspaper could use a readable, helpful advice column—which I would be happy to write.

"We can't afford another feature," he stated with finality.

"But I'll write it for nothing—as a public service," I countered.

"Sorry, not interested," he said, rising from his chair, which was my cue to leave. So I left.

Returning home, crestfallen, I began to think about the advice column I had been reading every morning in the *San Francisco Chronicle*. The more I thought about it, the more convinced I became that I could do a better job, so I impulsively rang up the *Chronicle* and asked for the feature editor.

Much to my surprise I was put through immediately to one Stanleigh Arnold.

Identifying myself as a Hillsborough housewife, I asked if he would see me for five minutes so I could present an "interesting proposition."

"What about?" he snapped.

"About that advice column you're running," I snapped back. "It's pretty grim."

"And I suppose *you* can write a better one," said the short-fused editor. "Fall in line. A lot of people tell me that."

"Then maybe it's time you listened," was my brash reply.

"Well," said Arnold, trying to terminate the conversation as courteously as possible, "if you're ever in the neighborhood, come in and see me." (End of conversation.)

The next morning I headed for the city in my chauffeur-driven car, judiciously leaving it around the corner from the *Chronicle*. (I didn't want anyone to think I was a well-heeled society woman who wanted a job to relieve my boredom for a month or two.)

The *Chronicle* was a beehive of activity—telephones ringing, typewriters clacking, and a lot of busy-looking people each doing his own thing.

I finally located Arnold in his glass cage off the city room. He was shouting instructions into the phone. I stood self-consciously in front of his desk, feeling very much as if I didn't belong there.

Arnold completed his telephone conversation, stood—all six-foot-five of him—extending a big, ham-like hand, and said, "I'm Auk Arnold. What's on your mind?"

I told him that I was the Hillsborough housewife who had called him yesterday about the advice column.

"What newspapers have you written for?" he asked.

I told him that although I had never written profes-sionally, I had taken all the journalism and psychology that my little college back in Sioux City had to offer. Then I recited the long list of volunteer organizations for which I had worked. He was visibly underwhelmed.

Just to get rid of me, he loaded my arms with old copies of the *Chronicle*, told me to substitute my answers to letters that had appeared in the advice column, and come back—in about a week.

I went directly to my husband's office not far from the *Chronicle*, commandeered a typewriter, and whacked out my answers. They were mostly flip, saucy one-liners.

Two hours later I was back at the *Chronicle* rattling Auk Arnold's cage. This time, however, he was too busy to see me, and a secretary asked me to leave my work (together with my name and phone number). I was given the old "Don't call us—we'll call you" treatment.

The drive from San Francisco to my home took less than an hour. As I opened my door, the phone was ringing. It was Mr. Arnold. The brass at the *Chronicle* was interested in seeing me again.

I returned to the *Chronicle* and learned that the sample was ample. They were going to give me a chance!

That evening I told my husband about the column I

might be writing for the *Chronicle.* Then he gave me the most valuable business advice I've ever had: "If you plan to write professionally, copyright your pen name and own it yourself."

The name, of course, was Abigail Van Buren. I took the "Abigail" from the Old Testament, for Abigail was a prophetess in the Book of Samuel, and it was said of her, "Blessed are thou, and blessed is thy advice, O Abigail." For my last name I chose "Van Buren" from our eighth president Martin Van Buren, because I liked the aristocratic, old-family ring.

The column was named "Dear Abby."

When salary was discussed, I offered to write it for nothing—as a public service.

"Oh, we have to pay you *something,*" they insisted, so I said, "How about twenty dollars a week?" And they said, "Sold!"

I immediately called my twin in Chicago to tell her that I had been hired to write the advice column for the *San Francisco Chronicle.* She said, "Congratulations, that's marvelous. I'm so happy for you!" And I knew she meant it.

So on January 9, 1956, with my participles dangling and my infinitives splitting, I was launched in my writing career.

You've heard about the kid who sent out a lot of invitations to his birthday party and was heartbroken when nobody showed up? Well, that's nothing compared to the insecure feelings of a brand-new advice columnist who wonders, "What if nobody writes in?"

I need not have worried. The early trickle of letters became a cascade. Within two weeks it became obvious that I needed secretarial assistance, so I placed an ad in the *San Mateo Times* hoping to find a competent "ex-secretary" who lived near me and could be lured out of retirement to give me a hand.

My first applicant, Kathleen Beal, filled the bill to perfection. I hired her on the spot, and she's still with me as my assistant, right arm, and cherished friend.

"Dear Abby" had been in print only a few months when the publisher of the *New York Mirror* called to say he had seen my column in the *Chronicle* and wanted it for his newspaper as soon as he could get it!

Having no agent or business manager (I still haven't), I discussed the *New York Mirror* offer with my husband. He saw no reason why "Dear Abby" shouldn't appear in the *New York Mirror*. I certainly wasn't competing with my twin, because her column did not run in New York City.

Knowing less than nothing about "syndicates" and how they operated, I sought advice from my bosses at the *San Francisco Chronicle*. They recommended that I sign with "McNaught," a New York syndicate whose representatives just happened to be in town at the moment.

Let me say here that I had been perfectly content to write exclusively for the *Chronicle*, and had I not been offered the *New York Mirror*, the thought of syndication would never have crossed my mind.

My exposure in New York created a minor sensation, and soon I was getting letters from editors around the country asking *me* how they could get my column.

"Dear Abby" was heralded as "a phenomenon in modern journalism—the fastest rising star in the business."

I became an instant celebrity. When Edward R. Murrow, the famous radio-television commentator, asked if he could televise me and my family from our home in Hillsborough on "Person to Person," I felt that I had really arrived.

After my appearance with Ed Murrow, my career shot upward to undreamed-of heights, and "Dear Abby" was soon being read by more people in more languages than any other newspaper column in the history of journalism.

Meanwhile back in Chicago, the Ann Landers list of newspapers was growing proportionately, because nearly every city had two newspapers, and when Abby went into one Ann went into the other. However, I was soon to feel an unmistakably cool breeze from the windy city of Chicago. The Chicago Sun-Times Syndicate looked upon "Dear Abby" as formidable competition, and they blamed Ann for introducing her twin sister to the lovelorn field.

My twin felt betrayed because I became syndicated. I insisted that the world was big enough for two good advice columns and tried desperately to make her see it my way. I wasn't getting through to her.

Contrary to reports, there never was a time when my twin and I were "not speaking," but I must admit that our once close and loving relationship was badly damaged.

While relatives and friends tried desperately to bring us together, national magazines poured fuel on the fire by publishing the "feud" between America's two top advice-givers.

We both steadfastly denied the reports that we were feuding. I dismissed such rumors with a typical Abby quip: "If you want a place in the sun, you've got to put up with a few blisters." In retrospect, I'm not very proud of those days.

For seven years my career flourished, but I walked around with a hole in my heart. There wasn't a day that I didn't miss my twin and I wrote countless letters telling her so. I even sent her an olive branch once, but she remained distant. As time went by, a reconciliation seemed hopeless.

Then suddenly, on May 4, 1964, my telephone rang, and then I heard that husky voice so like my own say, "Hello, Popo—This is Eppie." My heart started to pound and my throat closed up. I couldn't talk.

Then she asked, "Do you and Mort have any plans for your twenty-fifth wedding anniversary?" (It was hers, too, since we were married together.)

When I finally found my voice I told her that we had been thinking about going to Bermuda for a few weeks.

"Shall we make it a foursome?" she asked.

It took me all of one second to say, "Yes!"

And thus began the reuniting of a pair of identical twins who together have cornered the largest supermarket confessional in the world.

Marriage on The Rocks

Back in Biblical times, a man could have as many wives as he could afford. Just like now.

The first recorded divorce was granted in Babylon in 2250 B.C. In those days, if a husband became bored, he simply told his wife to get lost.

In time, the institution of marriage became stronger, and both parties took the vow to stay together "in sickness or in health, for richer or poorer, 'til death do us part."

A divorce was difficult to obtain—but not impossible. As one notorious divorce lawyer used to ask his clients, "Will you provide the evidence, or shall we?"

However, in the last twenty-five years everything has become easier. Especially divorce.

Today, in many states, when couples split they don't need grounds. They simply "dissolve" the marriage.

Abby advice circa 1956 would have urged couples to hang in there at all costs to try to save the marriage. Today I no longer feel that way.

Divorce almost always leaves scars. But when the joy

has gone out of a marriage and the joyless couple is faced with a choice of evils, divorce is usually the lesser of the two. My change of mind did not go unnoticed:

DEAR ABBY: What has happened to you? You used to encourage married couples to do everything within their power to save their marriages. Lately, you give the impression that divorce could be the answer for some couples. Why?

FAITHFUL READER

DEAR READER: Because I think it's more important to save people than marriages. And in some cases, in an effort to save a marriage that isn't worth saving, people have destroyed themselves and each other.

It is now considered the "in" thing for divorced couples to take a more "civilized" attitude toward their replacements.

I'm all for letting bygones be bygones, but some of my readers suggested that the original Mrs. Joe Doe done went and overdid it:

DEAR ABBY: I recently received an invitation which read: "The *old* Mrs. John Doe requests the pleasure of your company at cocktails and supper for the *new* Mrs. John Doe, etc."

It floored me. I knew our friends John and Mary Doe had gotten a quickie Mexican divorce, and it was rumored that John was interested in a lady from New York, but how about this?

Abby, is it normal for an ex-wife to be such a good sport?

SHOCKED

I told "shocked" that it wasn't necessarily normal, but I found it rather refreshing.

Other good sports wrote in:

DEAR ABBY: A woman was "shocked" to receive an invitation to a cocktail party from "The old Mrs. John Doe" to meet "The new Mrs. John Doe."

Well, what would she have thought of me? My ex-husband and his new wife lived with my new husband and me for four months because they were broke. Next Saturday I am giving a baby shower for my ex-husband's bride, who is due in two weeks. We get along very well—all four of us. I just wanted you to know that "good sports" like us are not as rare as you may think.

"GOOD SPORT" IN BERKELEY

DEAR ABBY: What's so "sporting" about a divorcee giving a party to introduce her ex-husband's new wife? I am a divorced man, and for years I have been looking for some nice guy who will marry my ex-wife. Believe me, if I ever find one I will throw a party for the two of them the likes of which this town has never seen. Sign me, "Another good sport in Beverly Hills," or. . .

SICK OF ALIMONY

— ♥ —

Then there are those who are so "civilized" about divorce even their closest friends are nonplussed:

DEAR ABBY: I will never again say that a letter in your column is too unbelievable to be real. Listen to this:

My husband and I recently attended the twenty-fifth wedding anniversary party of a couple we had known for years. It was a beautiful dinner party at a club for about a hundred guests.

Around midnight, the husband said that he and his wife had an announcement to make. They stood arm in arm, and he said, "We've had twenty-five years of marriage. Our children are married now, and there is no longer a reason to go on pretending our marriage is a success. It has been a failure for many years, so we've decided that while we are both young enough to enjoy life, we're getting divorced. It's nobody's 'fault.' It's mutual and friendly and we hope you will continue to be our friends."

They kissed each other and danced together as the band played, "Good Night, Sweetheart."

Can anybody top this?

WAS THERE

My terse reply: I hope not.

— ♥ —

But somebody did:

DEAR ABBY: I think I can top the story about the couple who at their twenty-fifth wedding anniversary party announced that they were getting a divorce.

On Sunday, March 5 of this year, our minister announced from the pulpit that he was leaving in June for a new assignment. He said that he and his wife were being divorced, after which he would marry a local medical doctor's wife. He said the doctor, who was standing beside him in the pulpit, would marry his wife. (There were five children involved.)

The minister and his wife had sung a duet that morning, and the doctor, who was a church official, had read the Scriptures for the service.

This is absolutely true. I witnessed it, and am enclosing the names of all the parties involved if you want to check it out. Being unable to stay in such a church, I left it immediately and joined another one.

"TOPPER" IN TAFT, CALIF.

Then wouldn't you know somebody topped the topper:

DEAR ABBY: If I did not witness this myself, I would never have believed it, but this is what happened:

A prominent couple we know invited us to their fiftieth wedding anniversary party, which was held at a stylish country club. There were about two hundred guests.

After the dinner, the son-in-law, who was the toastmaster, toasted the honored couple and called on his father-in-law to say a few words. The father-in-law got up and said, "I have an announcement to make. The last twenty-five years I have been living in hell. Ida wanted to go to Palm Springs every winter and I wanted to go to Miami. We always went to Palm Springs. Ida liked to play cards, I preferred to go to the races. We always played cards. There were other differences too numerous to mention. I don't know how much longer I have to live, but I have decided to spend my last years in peace—doing what I want to do.

"Ida can also do what she wants to do, as she is well

provided for. If she wants a divorce she can have it, plus half my assets. I'll settle for a separation. I'm not drunk. And I'm not mad. I'm just being honest. Thank you!" Then he sat down. Everybody was flabbergasted. Some thought he was kidding.

Well, he wasn't. He and Ida are now living apart. She's in Palm Springs and he's in Miami.

WITNESS

Whether or not to stay married for the sake of the children is always a hard decision. But some "children" make unreasonable demands on their parents:

DEAR ABBY: I am absolutely beside myself with the news my parents gave me this morning. They drove over here and calmly announced that after forty-four years of marriage they are getting a divorce! I honestly believe they have taken leave of their senses.

They have had their differences like all married couples, but they have never separated—not even for one day. I can't imagine what has come over them.

Dad says that since he is seventy, if the good Lord gives him another five years he wants to live them in peace. Mother, who is sixty-nine, says she feels the same way.

I suggested a larger apartment with two bedrooms, frequent separate vacations, a trial separation—anything but divorce. But they insist they have thought it over and this is what they both want. Abby, they have children and grandchildren who love and respect them. How can parents disgrace their families that way?

THEIR DAUGHTER

DEAR DAUGHTER: Your parents have a right to make their

own decisions, for their own reasons, without loss of love or respect from their children and grandchildren. And if they terminate their marriage after forty-four years, where is the "disgrace"? Perhaps they stayed together as long as they did out of consideration for you. They need compassion, not criticism.

— ♥ —

DEAR ABBY: What do you think of parents who have decided to call it quits after fifty-one years of marriage? They have four married children, thirteen grandchildren, and three great-grandchildren. They were never exactly lovebirds, but it never came to a real separation before.

I am the eldest daughter and Mama called me and told me to come and get her, as Papa had moved to a motel and she wasn't going to stay in the house alone. It's been three days, and Papa is still holed up in the motel.

My oldest brother telephoned Papa and asked what he should tell people. Papa said, "Tell them I've entered my second childhood and I have the measles!" Then he slammed down the telephone. So what should we tell people?

EMBARRASSED

I told "Embarrassed" that Papa's explanation would do.

Unfortunately, most divorces leave at least one party badly hurt, and it's hard for the injured party to accept the fact that the marriage can't be mended.

DEAR ABBY: I am married to a man I love with all my heart. He says he no longer loves me and he wants a divorce. We have three children. At first he said there was no one else and he just wanted to be free, then after I begged him to reconsider, he admitted there was another woman.

I would get down on my hands and knees if I thought it would do any good. I tried to tell him how much I loved him. I even kissed him, but he stood there like a statue with his hands in his pockets. Abby, I am desperate. How can I get him to love me again? The divorce is coming up soon in court. No fault. No chance. Help me. I don't want to live without him.

ALONE AND CRYING

DEAR ALONE: You aren't alone. You have three children, which are three good reasons for living.

Since there is another woman in the picture, your chances for making him "love you" again are zilch. Furthermore, there is nothing less appealing to a man than a begging, prideless woman. So dry your tears, square your shoulders, and chin up. Concentrate on making a new life for yourself. Sometimes good luck comes disguised as disaster.

My mail tells me that when the children in a divorce are minors, the child-support issue is major:

DEAR ABBY: So much has been said about "louses" who are late with the support check, I'd like to say a few words about the other side.

My husband was stationed in Alaska when his first wife started running around. By the time he got home it was too late to save his marriage—or his credit rating. When the case came to court, he was a "gentleman" and didn't use the grounds of adultery, so the judge gave his wife custody of their four children, plus support payments.

Two days after we were married his wife shipped the kids to us for their "summer vacation." She came to pick them up twenty-six months later! During that time we had a child of our own and a second one on the way.

Whenever she gets tired of the kids she ships them to us. They are always shoeless, threadbare and starved for a decent meal. Their support money is obviously used for something else.

I believe a divorced man should support his children, but this is ridiculous.

THE OTHER SIDE

Some people love to tell a friend that her husband has a "side-dish." Others rush to supply the ingredients after a divorce. In either case, it's bad taste:

DEAR ABBY: After nearly ten years of marriage, and two lovely children, my husband and I are getting a divorce.

We never washed our dirty linen in public. In fact, we had a good social life and everyone thought we were a very happy couple.

My problem: Since the news of our divorce has become public, many of our friends have called to tell me how "smart" I am to call it quits. They say they have known for years that my husband was fooling around, and then they proceed to fill me in on all the sordid details.

What am I supposed to say? I surely can't thank them for pouring salt on my wounds with all these ugly details.

ACHING HEART

DEAR ACHING: Those who would pour salt on your wounds aren't friends. In the future, when someone begins to fill you in, say, "Thanks, but I'm not interested."

DEAR ABBY: My husband was the "quiet type"—the last person in the world anyone would suspect capable of infidelity. Nevertheless he was.

I caught him with his girlfriend right in our own bed when I came home unexpectedly from a trip.

After I filed for divorce, three of my neighbors told me that for the last year they had seen this young woman entering and leaving my home many times after I had left for work.

I wanted to scream, "Why didn't you tell me? You could have spared me all this!"

Then I realized that they probably thought they were doing "the right thing" by keeping quiet. Abby, had I been told, perhaps it could have been ironed out by counseling; or just knowing would have caused me to file for divorce and be spared the humiliation of walking in on such a scene.

THE LAST TO KNOW

DEAR LAST: I would not advise anyone to inform on his neighbors. There is too much margin for error. The word from here is to keep your lip zipped.

To split or not to split. That is the question I am asked over and over again. Often the writer knows the answer and just wants an objective reading of the situation:

DEAR ABBY: Three years ago I married for a second time, thinking I would have companionship for the rest of my life, but I was wrong. All Carl wanted was a cook and housekeeper. He always wants to go to visit his children and grandchildren. Never mine. Not only that, but he is very close with a dollar. He has a lot more than I have, and he doesn't spend any of his. Only mine. We live in my house, and I pay the taxes and upkeep while he hangs on to his money which he will leave to his children. I am sixty-four. What would you advise—a separation?

NETTIE

DEAR NETTIE: A separation—of money, for openers. If Carl has money, let him spend it. Talk in money-syllables. If he isn't any happier with this arrangement than you are, then separate everything else.

DEAR ABBY: I am a twenty-nine-year-old woman who has married and divorced the same man three times in the last ten years. Our last divorce became final three weeks ago, and now Mike is begging me to marry him again. We have no children, and we don't want any. Abby, the only time he is decent to me is when we're divorced. He's a wonderful lover but a rotten husband. He's a boozer and a cheater.

If I told you how much we've spent on lawyers you would think we were out of our minds. I love the guy but I know if I marry him again he'll go back to his old abusive ways. Can you help me?

THREE-TIME LOSER

DEAR LOSER: Three strikes and a man is out, no matter how good his pitches. Some men are great to date but not to mate, and Mike could be one of them.

It all goes to show that some people take their marriage-on-the-rocks with a twist of lemon and some with a dash of bitters. However you take it, divorce is hard to swallow.

DEAR ABBY: My husband's former wife, Velma, with whom we have remained on fairly good terms, invited us to her home for a party. She is now married to a very well-to-do man.

Velma told me it was going to be a costume party, so my husband and I dressed up like a couple of rabbits.

Imagine our surprise when the butler opened the door and ushered us into a room filled with men in tuxedos and women in stunning gowns! We felt like a couple of fools. Velma laughed and said she thought it was funny. I was very upset to have been made the butt of her joke, so I got myself a glass of punch and spilled it on her gown. Then I laughed and told her I thought it was funny. However, she didn't see anything funny about it.

My husband isn't speaking to me, and he thinks I owe Velma an apology. What should I do?

A WIFE IN NEED

I replied: "Send Velma a bunch of carrots, and tell her you're sorry."

Roll Over, You're Snoring

I have long suspected that more people are sleeping apart because of snoring than are sleeping together for all the other reasons combined. A few years ago I received a plea for help signed "Frantic in Fresno":

DEAR ABBY: I woke up at three o'clock this morning, wondering who was mowing our lawn. Another time I dreamed a tugboat was stuck in our bedroom, frantically signaling for help. This has been going on for fifteen years, Abby. I can't remember the last time I had a good night's sleep. When I threaten to go into another bedroom, my husband says he didn't marry me to sleep alone. I have begged him to see a doctor or to try remedies I have heard about. But he won't. He says I snore. Can you help me?

FRANTIC IN FRESNO

On a hunch, I published "Frantic's" letter in my column, asking for readers' comments. I received more than five thousand replies. Some offered "cures," but most came from writers who reported years of anguished sleeplessness.

More than 90 percent of those who answered said that they had begun sleeping apart from their mates the moment another bed became available. I learned that love may be blind, but it's not deaf. One writer wrote:

DEAR ABBY: For nine years I have endured the most unbelievable racket. My husband not only snores, he grunts, groans, whistles, jerks and mumbles. When I tell him about it later, he denies having made a sound and accuses *me* of having nightmares.

GOING CRAZY IN OAKLAND

The wife of a New York stock broker is not in the market for amorous antics from her snorer:

DEAR ABBY: Not only does my husband snore, he grinds his teeth in his sleep and gives me financial reports all night long. If I wake him up, he gets passionate. Now really, after twenty-six years, who needs *that*?

NO NAME, PLEASE

Another victim discovered her problem on her wedding night. But she fortunately found a solution, which she insists saved her marriage.

DEAR ABBY: I'll never forget the first night of my honeymoon. My darling fell fast asleep at midnight while I was awake until seven o'clock the next morning just listening to him snore. He started out by holding his breath for so long I didn't know whether to send for a doctor or a priest. Then he'd exhale ever so slowly, emitting a long whistle, popping his lips and finally terminating with a noise that sounded like a corps of pneumatic drills. I felt like kicking him right through the wall every night.

After the honeymoon we got twin beds. That didn't solve anything. It just made it harder for me to kick him. Finally, we had separate bedrooms, but I could hear him through the walls. Then a friend introduced me to the greatest invention since sliced bread. Ear plugs! They have saved my marriage, and I am not kidding.

HELEN B. IN ST. PAUL

Another bride with a snoring groom offers yet another solution:

DEAR ABBY: On our honeymoon I was horrified to discover that I had married the world's champion snorer. I used elbows and feet for temporary relief. Now we sleep in twin beds and I keep a yardstick under my bed. When Michael starts snoring, I get the yardstick and whack him with it. Now, as soon as he hears me reaching for the yardstick, he shuts up.

MICHAEL'S WIFE

And from Chicago:

DEAR ABBY: I spent fourteen years listening to my husband snore, while I hung onto the side of the bed to keep as far away from him as possible. Herbert is the affectionate type. He kept reaching for me, and when he'd find me he'd snuggle up and snore right into my ear. I eventually learned to yield my side of the bed and walk around and get into bed on the other side. But after ten or twelve round trips per night, believe me, I am a pretty tired woman.

WINDED IN THE WINDY CITY

A Syracuse wife wrote that medical science hasn't been much of a help to her:

DEAR ABBY: My husband doesn't just snore. It's a combination of things he does with his nose, throat and teeth. Besides that, he steps on the brake all night. I finally sent him to an ear, nose and throat specialist with orders to do something—or else. Guess what the doctor told him. "Look, if I knew a cure for snoring, I'd use it myself. I am the world's worst. My wife refuses to go on vacations with me unless we take two rooms—on separate floors!"

Sign me

STUCK IN SYRACUSE

Our friendly neighbors to the north were heard from:

DEAR ABBY: I am convinced that the most idiotic thing I ever did in my life was to put up with Ralph's snoring as long as I did.

For years I walked around half-dead from exhaustion. Once, when I was near total collapse from lack of sleep, I spent the night in our guest room. The next morning the children whined, "Don't you love Daddy anymore?" So like a fool I felt I had to stay in the same room with that mountain lion to keep the children happy. What a lot of utter nonsense. No more! I'm older now and wiser.

HAD IT IN WINNIPEG

DEAR ABBY: When I was a young girl I had to cut across a cow pasture to get to school. A couple of cows chased me once, making those terrible mooing noises, and I have been terrified of cows ever since.

I've been married a short time, and lately have been having horrible nightmares about those cows. Then I discovered that my husband's snoring brought back the memory of those pursuing cows. We have a very small apartment so I can't go into another bedroom to sleep. How does a wife sleep with a husband who snores?

EXHAUSTED IN TORONTO

DEAR ABBY: My husband has snored off and on for thirty-three years and I wouldn't think of trying to cure him. You see, Albert snores only when he has a guilty conscience. After having been kept awake most of the night because he's snored up a storm, I cross-examine him. And sure enough—he's been up to something. Either women or gambling. He's almost sixty now and he's cut down on his snoring. I presume he has less to feel guilty about. I'm sure he still gambles, however.

MURIEL IN MONTREAL

DEAR ABBY: If only my husband snored in his sleep, I'd be happy. He thrashes around, kicks, hollers, grinds his teeth, and swings his fists. I was always black and blue and a nervous wreck from lack of sleep. I went to a doctor and he prescribed tranquilizers for my husband. He refused to take them, so I take them, and it helps a lot.

TRANQUILIZED IN VANCOUVER

Nothing worked for this long-suffering sister:

DEAR ABBY: If you come up with a remedy for snoring, let me know. I've tried everything. The plastic earplugs almost punctured my eardrums, and the beeswax fell out of my ears and stuck in my hair. My doctor gave me sleeping pills but I'm afraid I'll become addicted. Believe it or not, my husband is a policeman and he is afraid to sleep alone. If I slip out and sleep on the couch, he comes looking for me. This "hero" is fifty-six years old.

BELLA IN BROOKLYN

A physician who is a well-known ear, nose, and throat specialist informed me that in some snorers the sound is caused by the flow of air that vibrates the soft palate and tissues that are close to the throat lining. When air is drawn in and expelled through *both* nose and mouth, in certain individuals the membranes vibrate noisily between the twin air currents. Snoring can also be caused, the doctor said, by a deviated nasal septum, a partial blockage of the breathing passage by small, grape-size growths known as polyps, or any malformation of jaws which forces breathing by mouth. Some of this can be corrected by surgery, orthodontics, or devices to keep the mouth closed.

Women, the doctor said, snore too. But, according to my survey, men outsnore the ladies 60-to-1. And almost every man who wrote to report a snoring wife added, "But you could never get her to admit it." For some strange reason if a woman is accused of snoring, she takes it as a personal insult.

There are some exceptions, however, like Lena, now in her seventies, who admits that she's been snoring up a storm since she was a girl:

DEAR ABBY: I've been snoring for at least sixty years. When I was ten I went to summer camp for two weeks. I snored so loud, nobody wanted me in their cabin, so every night they moved me somewhere else.

I'll never forget my first overnight train trip. I was nineteen and had never slept in a berth before.

I was sleeping peacefully when I was rudely awakened by the harsh voice of the Pullman conductor demanding that I get that man out of my berth!

LENA IN PASADENA

And now, a testimony to the tape recorder technique:

DEAR ABBY: Shortly after I married Mark I discovered that he snored. When I told him he snored, he denied it. Abby, his snoring sounded like a chicken bone in a garbage disposal!

Finally I decided I had had enough of his denials, so I bought a tape recorder and learned how to use it. One night after Mark fell asleep, I held the microphone under his nose and got about ten minutes of snoring. Then I reversed the tape, turned up the volume and nearly blasted him out of bed. (Thank heavens he didn't hit me.)

Only after I threatened him with a nightly rerun did he agree to see an ear, nose, and throat specialist for an examination. The doctor discovered several polyps (small growths) in Mark's nose, which he said could be the cause of his snoring. The polyps were removed in a simple surgical procedure, and now my darling snores no more! Pass this on.

PEACE AT LAST

DEAR PEACE: Not all snoring is due to growths in the nose, but it's well worth a trip to a doctor to find out.

— ♥ —

The plea for noctural togetherness, no matter what, came from a reader who regretted her choice:

DEAR ABBY: When our family decreased and there was a spare bedroom available, I took it over because my husband's snoring disturbed my sleep.

It was like closing the door on an intimacy of thirty-one years. Well, Abby, after five years of sleeping apart, my advice to a young bride is, "Don't, under any circumstances, take a room by yourself. Stuff your ears, put a pillow over your head, take a sleeping pill, but don't leave his bed. And don't let him leave yours."

Take it from a fifty-eight-year-old woman. Something dies when a man and his wife quit sleeping together. I can't explain it. It's not sex, either. It's something more important. And you'll never get it back. I know. I've tried.

Foolish

More than three hundred patents for antisnoring devices have been granted by the United States Patent Office. They include garrote-like neckbands to keep the neck in a stretch position, adhesive coverings to keep the mouth closed, and chin straps with pronged attachments to keep the tongue flat. There is a music-box gadget to be clamped to the pajama jacket: The moment the sleeper turns over on his back—the favored snoring position—a low, soothing voice murmurs, "Roll over, darling." A St. Louis woman said it worked fine—for a while. Now she has returned to the more direct approach, and yells, "Dammit, Harry, shut up!"

Perhaps not in our time, but one day surely there will be a "cure" for snoring. Until it comes, take comfort from this letter:

DEAR ABBY: About snoring: That was my complaint three years ago, but I got over it when I read something in your column. It was, "Snoring is the sweetest music this side of heaven. Ask any widow."

4

The Traumatic Teens

Tucked away among the thundering "thou shalt nots" in the Mosaic code is a mild, positive commandment. It is interesting that it says "honor" thy father and mother. Nothing in there about love, or affection. Whether it is taken devoutly as the word of God or pragmatically as a guide to human conduct, the injunction is to duty only.

The full translation in the beautiful King James Version goes like this:

"Honor thy father and thy mother: that thy days may be long upon the land which the Lord thy God giveth thee."

"Honor," it says, and it posts the direction like a one-way street. Neither this commandment nor any other of the Ten Commandments enjoins parents to honor their children—or to love them.

Parenthood has always been fraught with troubles. But never more than in the last twenty-five years. Curiously enough, parents began hearing a lot about "love" from their children.

"Love" was the rallying cry of the young beatniks of the fifties and the drooping flower children who succeeded them.

If everybody would just love everybody else, everything would be lovely—so the message went.

In the sixties, we saw kids flaunt their contempt for the establishment and "phony" materialistic values by using X-rated language and wearing ragged clothing, long hair, and unkempt beards—and looking for all the world as if they were on their way to a meeting to overthrow the government. Perplexed parents were asked to understand their kids' experimentation with mind-altering drugs, sexual promiscuity, and other kooky conduct.

"Love!" they cried as they pitched bricks through the dean's window.

The war in Vietnam helped to widen the generation gap, although the counterculture had germinated before our country made the most serious mistake in its history. And as it turned out, the kids were right.

Some parents took the cue suggested in Victorian melodramas ("Go, and never darken my doorway again!"), but many more wisely tried to coexist with their rebellious young adult children by letting them do their own thing lest they risk total and permanent estrangement.

No one said raising children was easy, but in the last twenty-five years parenting has become a horrendous challenge.

Surely, no respectable middle-class parents of today ever expected to have a junkie in the family. That sort of thing was once reserved for the very rich or the very poor, not the stable, God-fearing middle class. I have received enough heartbreaking letters on this subject to fill another book. I always counsel love, patience, and very close attention by the parents to the activities of their wayward children—not expulsion. I also implore these guilt-ridden parents not to blame themselves for what happens in these permissive times. Peer pressure is often more persuasive than parent pressure.

Nowadays when kids go off to college, some take to "shacking up" with a member of the opposite sex. Most parents are understandably less than thrilled with this arrangement, but there is little they can do. Which poses another typical problem:

DEAR ABBY: Our son is a college senior, and he makes no secret of the fact that he and his girlfriend (also twenty-one) are shacking up near campus.

We disapprove of this sort of thing and he knows it, but he is now twenty-one and there is nothing we can do about it. Now for the problem: He asked if he could bring his girl home for Christmas vacation. We know they sleep together at school, but should we let them sleep together in our home?

My sister says, "Don't be a hypocrite. Even if you put them up in separate bedrooms, you know they'll manage to get together during the night anyway."

Maybe she's right, but I can't see putting them up together like a married couple in our guest room.

So, what do I do?

OLD-FASHIONED MOTHER

DEAR MOTHER: In your home, *you* make the rules.

If you disapprove of your son's lifestyle at school and he knows it, simply tell him there will be no shacking up under your roof. And he can either abide by the house rules or stay in a motel.

— ♥ —

I imagine some parents would settle for a kid who's "shacking up" in college rather than one like the son of "Had It in Schenectady" or the daughter of "Feeding an Elephant," whose letters follow:

DEAR ABBY: Our son was given every opportunity for as much education as he wanted, plus room and board without ever costing him a quarter, but as the kids say today, "He blew it."

Now he comes and goes as he pleases, lounges around the house, reading, listening to records, eating like a king, contributing nothing, and making long speeches about what is wrong with the world. We told him to get out until he either gets a job or goes back to school and completes his education. So far, neither alternative appeals to him.

He says that he is a minor and we have to take care of him until he is twenty-one. That means another eight months, and I don't think we can take it anymore. Any suggestions?

HAD IT IN SCHENECTADY

DEAR HAD IT: In Schenectady your son is an adult at eighteen, and he has no more right to live on your property than a stranger. You can give him the official thirty-days' notice to move out of your house, and if he refuses, the court will advise him that he has ten days to move, after which they will "help" him.

You don't live in Schenectady—you live in Atlanta, or Muscatine, Iowa, or Boston? Well, ring up your lawyer and find out what the law in your community says.

DEAR ABBY: How can parents get rid of a fat twenty-year-old daughter who refuses to look for a job? She says that we gave birth to her for reasons of our own, so we can keep her for the rest of her life.

Eating, sleeping, reading, listening to the radio, doing volunteer work at the local animal shelter, and urging her little brother to hang himself is all she has done since graduating from high school two and a half years ago.

Her skill with animals has brought her many good job offers from veterinarians, but she says she refuses to work for money as long as her brother is alive, and she fiercely resents not being an only child.

The police say they cannot help us because she is neither a criminal nor a lunatic. Two doctors have told us they cannot help us because they can't find anything "wrong" with her. So where do we go from here? We aren't millionaires and we're fed up with. . .

FEEDING AN ELEPHANT

DEAR FEEDING: See another doctor! This time find a competent psychiatrist or psychologist. You certainly have enough clues to conclude that the girl has serious emotional problems. She desperately needs help in getting her head together. And the cost will be "peanuts" compared with feeding an elephant.

A mother of teen-agers rebels and scores a victory for her side:

DEAR ABBY: I heard about teen-age rebellion, but I never experienced it until suddenly Joe, seventeen, and Betsy, fifteen, let me know they were "old enough to do as they pleased." Life became one constant battle about hair, clothes, late hours, and poor grades. Taking away privileges and cutting allowances didn't faze them. After I was told for the fiftieth time that they were old enough to do as they pleased, I saw the light.

I told them that by their reasoning I was also "old enough to do as I pleased." Then I sat down with a book, put my feet up, and relaxed. When they asked when dinner would be ready, I told them that whenever it pleased them they could make their own dinner. I then made myself a salad and a hamburger and continued to read my book, ignoring them.

For five days I neither cooked, cleaned, washed nor ironed for them. Only for myself. When they asked me what was wrong with me, I told them I was "old enough to do as I pleased" too, and it pleased me to think of no one but myself.

They finally got the point. Life is now restored to normal, and now we all live by the rules in this house. This may not work for everyone, but it worked for me.

REBELLIOUS MOTHER

— ♥ —

A fourteen-year-old Phoenix girl who "hated" her mother wrote to me about it. Her letter is typical of hundreds I receive daily, and so was my advice, which paid off—six years later.

DEAR ABBY: I am a fourteen-year-old girl and I hate my mother. It may sound terrible to you, but I really hate her. I used to think I would get over it, but I now know I never will.

Sometimes I think I will go out of my mind if she doesn't quit picking on me. I never do anything to suit her. She doesn't like my clothes, my hair, my friends, or anything.

My friends are not bums either. They are good kids and

mother says they look like trash. They aren't.

Please help me, Abby, before I run away from home. I cry myself to sleep at night because my mother is so hateful. If I baby-sit, she makes me put the money in the bank. Other girls can buy records or do whatever they want with the money they earn.

Don't tell me to talk to my father. He's always on her side. And don't tell me my mother "loves" me and is only doing things for my own good. If you print my letter, don't sign my name or I'll get killed.

MISERABLE IN PHOENIX

DEAR MISERABLE: Your letter doesn't shock me at all. I receive many such letters each week. Almost every normal teen-ager alternately loves and hates his parents.

It's not easy to be criticized, restricted, corrected, and disciplined day in and day out. But parents who really love their children prove it by consistently letting their children know what is expected of them. Parents who are "soft" and permissive rear confused, insecure children.

I don't expect you to agree with me today, but keep this letter and read it again three years from now, and then you'll understand it perfectly. Good luck, dear. You're lucky. You are loved.

DEAR ABBY: Now for my "P.S." I am no longer "Miserable." I am grateful.

I am twenty years old, Abby, and I just found the enclosed clipping tucked away in my diary. (I am "cleaning out my closets" because I am going to be married next June, and I'll be moving.)

You were so right. My parents were stricter than the parents of my friends, but now I realize that they set extra-high standards for me because they loved me and wanted me to be proud of myself.

I am saving that clipping to show my daughter if I am ever lucky enough to have one, because I intend to raise her just as my mother raised me, and she may "hate" me for the same reasons I "hated" my mother.

I am graduating from college in June and marrying a wonderful young man on the following Saturday.

How can I thank you?

"D" IN PHOENIX

I told "D" she already had.

— ♥ —

Thank heavens, the long-hair hassle is now a bad dream, but while it was raging, it was a nightmare:

DEAR ABBY: As I write this I am practically blinded by tears. My husband told our seventeen-year-old son that if he didn't come home with a haircut tonight, he didn't have to come home at all. It is midnight, and Jon is not home yet.

Why should something like the length of a boy's hair make such a big difference to a father? Jon is not a "bad" boy. All the boys he goes with have long hair.

Jon and his father have fought about this for over a year now. It has come to a showdown because he finally pushed the boy too far and gave him an ultimatum.

If something happens to Jon, I will never forgive my husband for his stubbornness.

I don't like long hair on boys either, but at least I didn't drive my own son out of the house because of it.

Please, say something about fathers who always have to have the last word. I have given up.

HEARTBROKEN MOTHER

DEAR MOTHER: There is much more involved here than

hair. In a good father-son relationship, the father never gives his seventeen-year-old an "ultimatum" merely because he "outranks" him. Patience and understanding should be forthcoming from the older and wiser man.

Tell Father to emphasize the more permanent and lasting aspects of his son's character and to forget the hair for now. It will grow shorter (or disappear entirely) soon enough.

The birth control pill, which became available not long after the "Dear Abby" column first appeared, has inspired a bale of mail. The most common inquiry from parents: Should I permit my underage daughter to use the pill? And from the daughter: Should I have to ask Mom and Pop for permission?

Many innocent third parties have been trapped in the generational conflict over the pill. Private physicians, members of the clergy, school counselors, and health-service administrators have been torn between the protests of parents and the demands of their children.

The questions arising from such explosive family confrontations should be answered, of course, on a one-to-one basis with the family involved. Since that is hardly practical in a widely distributed newspaper column, I have tried for a reasoned approach to the consequences of an untimely pregnancy. I think the baby deserves an inning.

DEAR ABBY: My telephone just rang. It was a doctor telling me that my sixteen-year-old daughter was just in his office asking for birth control pills. Abby, what are these young people doing to us mothers?

I knew she had a steady boyfriend, but I never dreamed

they were in need of anything like that. I am heartsick. I tried to raise the girl right. Where have I failed?

ASHAMED TO SIGN MY NAME

DEAR ASHAMED: You haven't failed, and if you tried to raise her right you need not be ashamed. I am not in favor of premarital sex for teen-agers, but once a girl has gone all the way it is unrealistic to think that she will stop simply because she is denied the pill. So then what? She risks becoming pregnant. And if she does, what has the doctor accomplished? He will have been responsible for (a) an unwanted baby, (b) an abortion, or (c) a hasty marriage. Which would you choose for your daughter?

If you are among those mothers who say, "If that's the way she is going to act, then let her suffer the consequences," please consider the baby. Don't you think every child should come into this world wanted by its natural mother? I do.

Here's a letter from a fifteen-year-old who exhibits some mature thinking. Refreshing!

DEAR ABBY: Recently you published a letter from a thirteen-year-old honor-roll student who thought she was mistreated because her mom told her what to wear, wouldn't let her wear make-up or have boys over, and generally treated her like a four-year-old.

Abby, please make it clear to teen-agers that while we are in our teens perhaps our parents should use even tighter restrictions on us. Our ideals and morals are just forming and we need the struggles with our authorities to strengthen us, but we don't always want to "win."

There is a story of a freshman scientist who watched as a butterfly struggled to be rid of its cocoon. Feeling sorry for it, the young scientist made tiny slits in the sides of the cocoon to ease the way. The butterfly soon emerged. But its wings were not fully developed (the struggle strengthens the wings) and it was unable to fly, so it died shortly thereafter.

Thank you, Abby, for letting another teen have her say.

"FIFTEEN, RESTRICTED, AND GLAD OF IT"

An authority on pot, I'm not. How much is still around? A lot.

DEAR ABBY: No one should drop in on his married children unannounced. They just might be smoking grass there!

I learned the hard way. If someone stole my purse, I'd report it to the police. But if I'm present when my children are smoking marijuana in their own homes, I just keep my mouth shut, leave, air out my clothes, and hope I never have to smell it again.

I know what I am going to put in their Christmas stockings next year. A hacksaw for her and a file for him.

I've invited my daughter, her husband, and several of their friends over for dinner next week, and if those kids light up in my house, I'll call the sheriff. (I wonder if I should warn them in advance? Or do you suppose after four years of college they are sufficiently educated to know that one doesn't break the law in the home of a host?)

I never thought I'd send a letter I couldn't sign, but here's one. Aren't we a bunch of lovely law-abiding Christian parents? Thanks for being a good ear. I had to tell someone or explode.

FRUSTRATED MOTHER

DEAR FRUSTRATED: Why the frustration? Just tell your kids you don't want them lighting up in your home, and if you are present when they light up elsewhere, you can always leave.

DEAR ABBY: Recently you printed a long list of penalties for being caught with marijuana, and since you made no comment, I assume that you believe these penalties are fair and just.

DISAPPOINTED READER

DEAR DISAPPOINTED: You are assuming a lot, my friend. I frequently publish letters without adding my comment. And many letters express views contrary to mine. I simply let others have their say. Why not? I don't assume that because someone disagrees with me, he is wrong and I am right.

I publish the legal penalties for being caught with marijuana because many are still unaware of what they have to lose. I also happen to feel that the punishment in some jurisdictions does not fit the "crime."

DEAR ABBY: Why do so many people say that pot is harmless? Our daughter began using it in January. She went on mescaline in March, started seeing a psychiatrist in May, and was in a mental hospital in July. She really had no intention of getting involved with drugs, but her nearest and dearest friend, a girl I liked and trusted, got her started. Now the mother of this girl says, "You know, I've been reading up on marijuana and it's really not so bad. It's no worse than tobacco or alcohol."

What can I possibly say to her? And to all the people

who are spreading this plague with their permissiveness?

CONCERNED

DEAR CONCERNED: While the most reliable authorities tell us that marijuana is no more addictive (habit-forming) than tobacco or alcohol, excessive use of pot can be as destructive to some individuals as excessive drinking and smoking is to others. There is no way of knowing who can "handle" such things and who cannot. Some people who drink like fish and smoke like chimneys live to be ninety. Others become alcoholics in their twenties and die of lung cancer in their thirties. It's a gamble. And of course the only winners are those who stay out of the game.

— ♥ —

Sometimes I regret not having studied law:

DEAR ABBY: Our fifteen-year-old, six-foot, two-hundred-pound son got a girl from a neighboring farm into trouble. She is also fifteen. We gave him strict orders to stay away from her, but it seems he didn't. Her people claim it's our fault.

I talked with a judge in the city, and he said there is a law that says if a man owns a bull, he is responsible for keeping the bull locked up. And if the bull gets loose and goes into a neighbor's pasture and breeds his dairy heifers, the owners of the heifers can't sue for damages because they should have kept their heifers locked up. My friend, the judge, says the same law applies to people. Do we have a case?

OHIO FARMER

DEAR FARMER: A man's son is not a bull; neither is his

neighbor's daughter a heifer. I can't practice law, but I think your friend, the judge, gave you a bum steer.

Well-meaning but misguided parents often grant themselves ethical immunity to snoop on their kids, to invade their privacy—all, of course, "for their own good."

DEAR ABBY: I can't quit thinking about what I did today and I've got to tell someone about it, so here goes. If you consider it wrong, I won't do it again.

I became suspicious and opened a letter my seventeen-year-old daughter received from her nineteen-year-old cousin who is in the service, stationed in a foreign country. It was full of explicit descriptions of sexual practices he said he had been indulging in—some I never knew existed. I tore it up before I even finished reading it. It was nauseating.

He also asked her to bake him some brownies with "grass" and send them to him without a return address on the box. I know "grass" is marijuana, but I never knew she had access to it.

Although I fully trust my daughter, I would shield her from the knowledge of such sexual practices as her cousin described. I am glad she will never read such trash, but I feel guilty about opening her mail.

Don't I have some rights as a parent to protect my daughter from unwanted, unwelcome information? Should I feel anxious about what she hears of abnormal sex practices? I lived all my life without this knowledge and still feel complete. She is the typical all-American girl, and I want to keep her mind pure and unadulterated. Am I wrong?

CONFUSED

DEAR CONFUSED: No one (parent or not) has the right to open another person's mail or destroy it. If the lines of communication had been opened between you and your daughter, you wouldn't have to resort to such acts to find out what kind of dialogue she has with her cousin. Judging from his letter, your daughter probably knows much more about sex than you think.

Even the most protective parents can't shield their children from the real world. All you can do is teach your daughter by daily influence and example what you think is right, moral or ethical, and let her make up her own mind.

DEAR ABBY: I needed some Scotch tape, so I looked in my son's desk for some and noticed the beginning of a letter my son had written to his girlfriend. It read, "I am only interested in being stoned, spending money, and sex."

I read no further.

My first impulse was to confront him with this, but he would say I had no right to go snooping through his desk.

I don't think I should go on ignoring this. I would appreciate some advice. He is eighteen-and-a-half.

BEWILDERED FATHER

DEAR FATHER: You could be about seventeen years too late. It won't help now to be reminded that you failed to build the kind of father-son relationship that inspires trust, confidence, and total honesty. It's possible that what you read did not reflect your son's thoughts accurately, however.

Don't tell him what you saw, but try to get a dialogue going so you can get inside his head. Encourage honesty, and no matter what he says, be cool and don't put him down or make him feel guilty. If you can develop candid two-way communication, you'll be able to influence and eventually help your son. He doesn't need punishment, Father, he needs a mature, understanding friend.

Some parents' discoveries don't come in the mail—clarity begins at home. Handling kids found in compromising positions can be a touchy situation, as in the following cases:

DEAR ABBY: Last Saturday night my husband and I went to the movies. Upon arriving home earlier than expected, we found our fifteen-year-old daughter on the couch with her boyfriend. They were all wrapped up in each other in a most disgusting position.

We ordered the boy out of the house and forbade our daughter ever to see him again. She flew into an angry rage and screamed that when two people are "in love" anything they did was "beautiful." She threatened to leave home if we don't let her see her boyfriend again.

What's a mother to do?

STUMPED

DEAR STUMPED: Try to be more understanding. Your daughter obviously doesn't know the difference between "love" and a healthy, normal, adolescent physical attraction. If you do, try to explain it to her. (If you don't, ask her to write to me and I'll try.)

You made a big mistake in ordering her boyfriend out of the house and forbidding your daughter ever to see him again. You should have had a frank talk with both of them about the hazards of intimacy. The boy should have been made to feel welcome in your home, but only on your terms. (You make the "rules" as to how often he may come, how late he may stay, etc.) If you drive them to meeting on the sneak elsewhere, you will create worse problems.

DEAR ABBY: Five months ago I hired a twenty-five-year-old buxom but pretty Scandinavian girl to live in and help with the cooking and cleaning. She proved to be a wonderful girl with a sweet disposition and the potential to be an excellent domestic.

Last Sunday my husband and I returned home earlier than we had anticipated. I went to this girl's room to tell her something, knowing she'd planned to stay home. Well, I found this girl and my seventeen-year-old son in a state of complete disarray and in the midst of a heated embrace.

My son said immediately, "Don't worry, Mom, we're in love and plan to get married as soon as I'm out of high school."

This is the most absurd idea we've ever heard of. We don't want to fire her because it might turn our son against us. He seems serious about this girl. Can you help us?

PERPLEXED

DEAR PERPLEXED: Apparently your son is under the impression that all a boy needs to get married is a girl who will say yes. You and his father ought to tell him about the birds and the bees and the lure of an "older" woman. And a couple of hundred other things concerning the difference between a solid marriage as opposed to a groovy Sunday afternoon.

A surprising reaction to the above letter came from a reader in Minneapolis:

DEAR ABBY: In regard to the mother who came home early on Sunday afternoon and caught her teen-age son and the young Scandinavian maid "in flagrante delicto":

You advised the mother to tell the boy about the birds and the bees. It would appear that the maid had already done that.

If the mother cans the maid, I would like to hire her. I love Scandinavian cooking.

LARS

The Homosexual Hassle

I am frequently asked, "Don't you think there's a lot more homosexuality today than there was twenty-five years ago?"

I can't answer that question and I doubt if anyone can, because twenty-five years ago it was against the law to be a homosexual. It still is in some places, which forces homosexuals to lead double lives, lest they lose their jobs, disgrace their families, and become social outcasts in a straight society.

In the last decade, however, closet doors have been swinging wide, and there has been a king-sized exodus of "closet queens." Some gay celebrities have proudly announced their emergence in magazine articles, in books, and on television talk shows. Others, not so famous, have merely dropped all pretenses, responding to the "Out of the closet!" rallying cry of the militant gays.

Homosexuals of both sexes are demanding equality with straights and protection under the law against discrimination because of their sexual preferences.

Most of us in the "straight" majority tend to go along with the titled English lady who said of odd sex practices that she didn't care what people did, just as long as they didn't frighten the horses.

Beyond this attitude of general tolerance, there are varying degrees of confusion, bewilderment, and despair on the parts of most parents and heterosexual mates of homosexuals.

"Gay and Hurting" wrote stating perhaps the most distressing problem among homosexuals:

DEAR ABBY: Thank you for trying to get parents to accept their homosexual children as they are. I'm sure my parents never would, and I'm almost having a nervous breakdown trying to keep it from them.

Abby, homosexuals need love and acceptance from their parents even more than heterosexual children do. But how can children ever hope to educate their parents? They read your column. Can you help?

GAY AND HURTING

In casting about for a way to help, I recalled the famous letter which Dr. Sigmund Freud once wrote in response to an anguished mother about her homosexual son.

Doctor Freud was old and ailing, but still practicing in Vienna the medical specialty of which he was the founder, psychoanalysis. Across the border in Germany, a rising dictator named Adolf Hitler had banned psychoanalysis and ordered the burning of Freud's books. But Freud felt secure in the civilized surroundings of Vienna. He had no way of knowing that within a brief three years it would require heavy international diplomacy to free him and his family from the Gestapo, and that he would die in London, a refugee.

Dr. Freud wrote this letter in 1935. He was seventy-nine, and we now see that his thinking was not only amazingly modern for his time, but also for ours. He was both precise and humane. He wrote as follows:

DEAR MRS._____,

I gather from your letter that your son is a homosexual. I am most impressed by the fact that you do not mention this term yourself in your information about him. May I question you, why you avoid it? Homosexuality is assuredly no advantage, but it is nothing to be ashamed of, no vice, no degradation, it cannot be classified as an illness; we consider it to be a variation of the sexual function produced by a certain arrest of sexual development.

Many highly respectable individuals of ancient and modern times have been homosexuals, several of the greatest men among them (Plato, Michelangelo, Leonardo da Vinci, etc.).

It is a great injustice to persecute homosexuality as a crime, and cruelty, too. If you do not believe me, read the books of Havelock Ellis.

By asking me if I can help, you mean, I suppose, if I can abolish homosexuality and make normal heterosexuality take its place. The answer is, in a general way, we cannot promise to achieve it. In a certain number of cases we succeed in developing the blighted germs of heterosexual tendencies which are present in every homosexual; in the majority of cases it is no more possible. It is a question of the quality and the age of the individual. The result of treatment cannot be predicted.

What analysis can do for your son runs in a different line. If he is unhappy, neurotic, torn by conflicts, inhibited in his social life, analysis may bring him harmony, peace of mind, full efficiency, whether he remains a homosexual or gets changed.

If you make up your mind he should have analysis with

me (I don't expect you will!!), he has to come over to Vienna. I have no intention of leaving here. However, don't neglect to give me your answer.

Sincerely yours with kindness,
FREUD

"DEAR HURTING," I wrote in my column, "perhaps if your parents read this classic letter from Doctor Freud it will help them to understand. I hope so."

It is worth noting that Freud seemed less concerned with the young man's homosexuality than with the possibility that treatment might help him to be a better adjusted person whether he remained a homosexual or not after analysis.

The entire matter of "curing" homosexuality is one that still causes lively debate whenever it arises.

I am reminded of a famous psychoanalyst who was asked how much success he had in "curing" homosexuals.

"Fifty percent of those I treated, I cured," he replied. Then quickly added, "I had only two patients. With one I succeeded and the other I failed."

Many parents have written to say that they were shocked, confused and torn to learn that a daughter or son of theirs was homosexual:

DEAR ABBY: Our tall, handsome, athletic son served four years in the Navy, returned to civilian life and college, and "married" an undersized, effeminate male hairdresser. We have no idea how to handle this situation or our ambivalent feelings.

This "odd couple" came to visit us, and they want us to visit them. They are inseparable and act out a peculiar husband-wife relationship that is both bewildering and disturbing to us.

So far we have been polite, but what the dickens do you say to friends and relatives? We can't condone it.

We love this boy, but as his parents we feel torn and hypocritical to say the least.

TORN

DEAR TORN: You owe friends and relatives no explanation, so don't feel obligated to offer any. Since your son's lifestyle bewilders and disturbs you, either learn to accept it or quit seeing him.

DEAR ABBY: The problem briefly: Our daughter (a good student at an out-of-town college) recently volunteered the information that she is a lesbian. We were stunned since we had no inkling of this.

After discussions and correspondence on the subject, she flatly refuses any form of counseling and says that she is happy at the present time and sees no need to change.

What more can we as parents do to keep her from ruining her life? We love her.

NEW YORKER

DEAR NEW YORKER: Why do you assume that her sexual preference will necessarily "ruin" her life? If you love her, accept her as she is and let her know it.

— ♥ —

My reply to "Torn" initiated a flood of letters. Many contained this theme:

DEAR ABBY: Your answer to "Torn" was perfect. If those parents really love their tall, handsome, athletic son, the best way to show it is to allow him to be himself, even if his choice of a life's companion is another man, and not the woman of their dreams.

I speak out of agonizing years of personal experience. I made my personal decision on the basis of what would please my parents, my friends, and society in general. I have tried to live a straight life in a straight world and have been relatively successful. But each day is an inner struggle. I have conformed to a way of life that is "proper," but it's unnatural for me. My life has been one long succession of unfulfilled yearnings.

I would advise any young person who is struggling with homosexual feelings to be true to himself. Thank God for the openness society is developing. Had I known twenty-five years ago that there could possibly be an alternative, I would have taken a different course.

Now, in my forties, I still wear a mask and am more miserable than ever.

Surely those parents wouldn't want that kind of misery for their son? Abby, please continue to tell parents that the opinions of their friends and relatives are not as important as their son's right to be himself.

UNHAPPY CONFORMIST

Following the publication of that exchange came letters from parents of homosexuals. Many damned me for my outrageous tolerance of homosexuality, and many quoted Scripture to support their protests.

Some even said they'd rather see their children *dead* than living in a homosexual union!

In the minority, however, were those like "Sad Mother" who wrote:

DEAR ABBY: Thank you so much for your words in defense of homosexuals. I am the mother of one, and I live in fear that one day he may take his own life. Most homosexuals feel that they were born that way and are not the product of their environment.

Please ask any one of your medical experts how easy it would be for him to turn himself into a *homosexual* if society demanded it.

I hope and pray that someday there will be a medical cure for these poor persecuted individuals.

SAD MOTHER

Militant gays bridle at the very notion that what they consider merely a sexual preference may be viewed by others as a kind of "sickness." I, for one, have always defended their rights to go their own way, as a sampling of the correspondence will show.

DEAR ABBY: I read with an aching heart the letter in your column from a woman who discovered after ten years and two children that her husband was homosexual. She has my heartfelt sympathy. I have lived in her situation for twenty years, the first ten trying to make it work and the second ten in hell.

If that woman is still young and can support her children, my advice to her would be to get out and never look back.

If she thinks things are bad now, wait until he gets older.

Her daily lot will be humiliation, loneliness, and fear of exposure. And she'll never know the luxury of being able to confide in a living soul.

The homosexual is a crippled personality in other ways than sex. This is not textbook talk, I've been there.

TWENTY-YEAR STRETCH

DEAR STRETCH: If, as you say, "a homosexual is a crippled personality," who can blame him? All his life he's heard that he's a "sick, perverted, abominable, loathsome creature," or some kind of freak. He has had to live like a criminal much of the time— for fear someone would "find out" about him. He feels guilty for having "failed" his family. (Is it any wonder the suicide rate for homosexuals is so high?)

I do not know whether homosexuals can be "cured." My medical experts insist that if they are sufficiently motivated, some can. But almost all my mail from homosexuals themselves says that the most they can hope for is "understanding" on the part of others, and the ability to accept themselves as they are and learn to live with it.

— ♥ —

DEAR ABBY: Recently you printed a letter from someone who claimed to be a "well-adjusted homosexual."

There is no such thing as a well-adjusted homosexual; the two terms are antonymous. Homosexuality, male or female, is a form of sexual deviation which is symptomatic of personality disorder. By any reasonable standard of human development, homosexuality is an abnormal human condition which needs competent professional treatment. It is, in effect, a form of emotional illness.

I think that you would be as interested as I in what your

readers think about the subject.

HAPPY HETEROSEXUAL

DEAR HAPPY: By whose definition is homosexuality an illness? There are homosexuals who live socially well-adjusted, discreet, personally happy lives, whose homosexuality would come as a surprise to many of their close heterosexual friends.

The fact that homosexuality is morally condemned by most people in our culture makes it seen abnormal. In other times and in other cultures it has not always been so judged.

Much of the maladjustment seen in homosexuals is due to the rejection, persecution, and guilt imposed on them by intolerant and ignorant contemporaries.

I arrived at my conclusions about homosexuality after many long discussions with the late Dr. Franz Alexander, a distinguished psychoanalyst whose friendship I cherished for many years. Alexander had been a student of Freud, so naturally he espoused Freud's theories, and I in turn espoused Alexander's.

Not all psychiatrists, however, agree with my views on the nature of homosexuality. Some insist that homosexuals are indeed "sick."

Another advice columnist has repeatedly stated that she supports that view, so a *Los Angeles Times* reader asked me to go on record as to where I stood on the controversy. He wrote:

DEAR ABBY: Another advice columnist keeps insisting that homosexuals are "sick." She says, and I quote:

"Thousands of homosexuals have written asking me where they can get 'straightened out,' so they must consider themselves sick—or they wouldn't be asking for help. Occasionally I hear from homosexuals who are at peace with themselves, but they are few and far between.

"I believe the majority of homosexuals would be straight if they were really free to choose."

What do you say, Dear Abby?

L.A. TIMES READER

My reply:

DEAR READER: I say if a heterosexual had been raised to believe that his preference for the opposite sex was "sick," twisted, abominable, sinful, and a disgrace to his family, he would ask for help on how to "straighten himself out," too.

Homosexuality is a problem because an unenlightened society has made it a problem, but I have received letters by the thousands (not just "occasionally") from gay people telling me that they wouldn't be straight if they had a choice. All they ask is to be allowed to love in their own way without facing the charge that they are "sick and twisted."

I say, love and let love.

— ♥ —

The widespread ignorance concerning homosexuality is indeed discouraging:

DEAR ABBY: As parents of a two-year-old boy, we are somewhat concerned about the following situation. We have a nephew (around thirty years old) who is a homosexual. This isn't just hearsay. He's a fine, talented, very nice person, but he just happens to be homosexual. Do you think we should ever let him alone with our son? Or would it be dangerous?

CONCERNED

I told "Concerned" as I had told hundreds of others who had expressed concern about similar situations that a homosexual was no more likely to molest a child than a heterosexual.

And speaking of ignorance, I have had to explain the differences between a homosexual, a transvestite, and a transsexual many times in my column. Briefly:

A homosexual is one whose sexual preference is for one of his or her own sex.

A transvestite is one who cross-dresses—occasionally, for the fun (or "thrill") of it, but is not necessarily a homosexual. In many instances, a transvestite is normal in every other respect, but enjoys wearing the attire of the opposite sex.

A transsexual is one who despises his (or her) sexual make-up and longs to be a member of the opposite sex. (Transsexuals are fond of saying, "I feel like a woman trapped in a man's body"—or "a man trapped in a woman's body.")

Sex reassignment surgery is now being performed in the United States, and transsexuals have come to be accepted and understood as they well should.

The phenomenon of married bisexuals was perhaps never so widely attested to as when the following letter appeared in my column:

DEAR ABBY: I have a Saturday job, but when our two boys went to visit their grandparents I decided to surprise my husband. I worked only half a day and hurried home. When I went into my bedroom I found Jim in bed with his best friend—a man! I couldn't believe my eyes. His friend (I'll call him Donald) left immediately and Jim and I had a long talk. He said he had always been gay, and married me (at nineteen) because he thought I could "cure" him, but he never stopped seeing men. Jim said he loves me but not as deeply as he loves Donald.

I never suspected a thing, Abby. We always had terrific sex, but I don't think I could ever sleep with him again. He's a loving husband and a great father and we had eighteen wonderful years. I don't hate him. I'm in total shock. What should I do? And what should I tell our sons?

DESPERATE WIFE

DEAR WIFE: Give Jim up graciously. He has already made a choice, either consciously or unconsciously. If your husband doesn't tell his sons the truth, you should tell them if they ask. No lies or cover-up. Bisexuality is a fact of life that can occur in any family.

Although my answer was (I believed) very well thought out, a surprising number of readers wrote to say that they were happily married to bisexual mates and that my advice was way out in left field!

DEAR ABBY: Your advice to "Desperate Wife," who came home early and found her husband in bed with his best friend (another male), was not very well thought out. You said, "Bisexuality is a fact of life that can occur in any family. Give him up graciously. He has already consciously or unconsciously made a choice."

Abby, if he has been a wonderful husband for eighteen years and a great father, as she stated, she should have been encouraged to try to save her marriage rather than demolish it.

Granted she is in shock, and granted there has been deception on his part, but she isn't the only woman in the world who's married to a gay man. If she lives in a big city, there is a mental health clinic and a gay community service agency that can put her and her husband in touch with a support group for gay married men and their wives. Counselors will help them deal with the realities of their marriage and show them how to build a new relationship based on honesty and open communication. Or they may conclude that it's best to separate. But at least they should consider the alternatives instead of escaping the marriage.

I am sorry that you viewed the situation as hopeless. It isn't.

GAY-LY MARRIED IN S.F.

DEAR ABBY: Your advice to "Desperate Wife," who had been happily married for eighteen years to a bisexual man, was simplistic.

Human beings are capable of more flexibility than you give them credit for. You didn't present any options. One was to help in adjusting to the idea that her husband is bisexual. She said they loved each other, had terrific sex, and great children. None of that has changed, nor has he changed. Only what she *knows* has changed.

My husband is gay, but we have come to realize that what we have together and what we give to each other and our children is more important than what happens when we are apart.

We can allow each other to live full and complete lives—whatever that may mean. You should have told that wife that leaving a loving husband isn't the only solution.

FOUND ANOTHER WAY IN MASS.

DEAR ABBY: As a neuro-psychiatrist, I have had many married bisexual patients. Most of them were vigorous, successful men in high-paying positions with intelligent, good-looking wives. In every case there also were healthy, well-adjusted children. There was a close rapport between these patients and their families for years until circumstances forced the skeletons out of the closet.

In every case the wife preferred to continue in the marriage. Not one man I ever treated was willing to give up his homosexuality—but he didn't want to give up his wife either. Such individuals seek help only when they get arrested, lose a lover, or are exposed for some reason.

L.A. PHYSICIAN

— ♥ —

On the gayer side of the gay controversy: It seems that unlike Ceasar's wife, no one is above suspicion—including Damon and Pythias, whose "brotherly" devotion to each other has been the talk of the last two centuries:

DEAR ABBY: My friend and I have a difference of opinion. He says Damon and Pythias were homosexuals. I say they were straight. Can you check this out and let us know?

C AND B

DEAR C AND B: I wrote to twelve leading universities. Their responses included yeses, noes, and maybes.

I think the chairman of the English Department at the University of Chicago summed it up very well:

"Dear Abby: You asked if Damon and Pythias were gay. In dealing with characters of such remote antiquity, who exist more in the realm of legend, it is sometimes difficult to find much evidence on the most intimate details of their private lives.

"Damon and Pythias were famous for their devotion to each other, and they were Greeks. Beyond that, I think whatever they did was pretty much their own business, and even if I knew, I wouldn't say.

"One less than eminent authority said to me, 'I think Damon was OK, but I'm not so sure about Pythias.'

Sincerely,
STUART M. TAVE"

— ♥ —

How much do you know about homosexuality? Mark the following statements "True" or "False."

1. Homosexuals commit more crimes than straight people. (True or False?)

2. Everyone is born straight, but some become gay because they have been seduced by a gay person early in life. (True or False?)

3. You can always tell homosexuals and lesbians by the way they act, dress, and talk. (True or False?)

4. If a person is gay, no amount of therapy or motivation can change him. (True or False?)

5. Boys raised by domineering mothers and weak (or absent) fathers usually turn into homosexuals. (True or False?)

6. Gay people can never become mothers or fathers. (True or False?)

7. Homosexuals are more inclined to molest children sexually than heterosexuals. (True or False?)

8. If a person has one or two sexual experiences with someone of the same sex he is gay. (True or False?)

9. The American Psychiatric Association stated that homosexuals are "sick." (True or False?)

10. Homosexuals can be legally married to each other under the law in the U.S.A. (True or False?)

11. Most homosexuals try to convert young people into becoming gay. (True or False?)

12. Children raised by gay parents (or gay people) usually become homosexuals themselves. (True or False?)

How did you score?

If you marked all twelve statements "False," you are very well informed.

If you marked nine statements "False," you are fairly well informed.

If you marked four or more statements "True," you have a great deal to learn about homosexuality, because all of the above statements are False!

One thing is certain, God made gays just as surely as He made straights. And all His children are entitled to live and love in dignity, without shame or guilt.

6

Sex: Too Much and Not Enough

The person who said "All men are created equal" never saw my mail.

And the inequality that most people write to me about is usually found in the bedroom. I refer to the vast disparity in sexual appetites.

According to my mail, the unequals are divided about equally into two categories: the sex-starved and the frigid-dears. What a pity I can't pair up those who feel cheated and those who would rather be left alone.

I am tempted at times, but my better judgment tells me that that kind of help would create more problems than it would solve.

For openers, some typical complaints from sex-starved women:

DEAR ABBY: I have a marriage license signed by two witnesses, so I must be married, although at times I'm not so sure. My husband has not come near me in I don't know how long. When I snuggle up to him for a little affection,

77

he says, "Don't bother me, I'm tired." Or, "Not now, it's too late."

I'm no slob, Abby. I'm attractive, clean, and I've kept my figure. I'm thirty-two and he's thirty-four and we both may as well be ninety.

I watch television in bed till my eyeballs fall out, but there's got to be more to marriage than this!

NO LOVE IN PITTSBURGH

A lady complains:

DEAR ABBY: I'm not saying this to boast, but I am twenty-five, my figure is 37-25-36, and I have won several beauty contests. Two years ago, I married what everyone (including myself) thought was a prize. He was thirty, handsome, college-educated, rosy future, etc.

Well, this "prize" has made love to me exactly five times in the last six months! I've tried every trick in the book. Once, I even gift-wrapped myself in Saran wrap and greeted him at the door with a martini. And he said, "Hi. What's for supper?"

I told him he should see a doctor to find out what's wrong with him, and he said I should see one to find out why I am never satisfied! Any suggestions?

PRACTICALLY UNTOUCHED IN TULSA

I told "Untouched" that she was tetched to put up with it. And that if her husband didn't see a doctor she should see a lawyer.

A reader was sufficiently touched by "Untouched's" letter to submit the following:

DEAR ABBY: I know it's impossible, but I would give a year's pay to meet "Practically Untouched," because I'm as hungry for affection as she is.

My wife is attractive, intelligent and fun to be with. I just can't get her into the bedroom.

If I retire early, she stays up watching television until I'm asleep. If I come home late from a business appointment, she's asleep—or pretends to be.

I am no slouch. I'm 6 feet 1 and weigh 180, fit as a fiddle, and have a headful of premature silver-gray hair. I play golf and tennis in summer and handball in winter.

I have never cheated on my wife. But I don't know how much longer I can curb my frustrations. I am constantly propositioned by women of all ages. Some of my wife's friends drop little hints. It's one big battle and not getting any easier. Sign me

ON THE VERGE

A reader signed "Doing All Right" offered "On the Verge" some practical pointers on the joy of sex:

DEAR ABBY: "On the Verge" complained because his wife was frigid.

Abby, you once said, "There are no cold women—only clumsy men." How right you were.

I am a man in my middle fifties. I'm short, balding, and slightly overweight, but I have been with plenty of women, and I have yet to find one that's frigid.

I am not saying this to brag, but once I make love to a woman I can't get rid of her. A woman needs to hear that she's desirable, lovable, and terrific. It's not so much what I *do*, it's what I say. A woman needs to hear that she's needed, wanted, and loved. If a woman is "frigid," it's because the man is selfish, impatient, and doesn't know how to turn her on.

DOING ALL RIGHT

DEAR DOING: You are living proof of what I have long contended. Words are a powerful aphrodisiac. If a woman hears the right things from her lover, he's got it (and her) made.

All right, we have heard about ear power, now let's hear it from *nose* power.

Granted, what one hears can turn a person off or on. But what one smells can also be a factor. Ladies first:

DEAR ABBY: What would you do with a man who refuses to use a deodorant, seldom bathes, and doesn't even own a toothbrush?

STINKY'S WIFE

DEAR WIFE: Absolutely nothing!

DEAR ABBY: My husband sleeps in his underwear. He wears the long woolen kind, and he sleeps in the same underwear he's worn all day. The problem is getting him to change it. Abby, there are four sets of clean underwear in his drawer, but he won't put on a clean pair without a fight. I can't even get the underwear away from him to put in the wash. Don't tell me to grab it when he's in the bathtub. He doesn't bathe much either. Please help me. He's getting pretty ripe.

HOLDING MY NOSE

DEAR HOLDING: Look at it this way. You don't have to worry about another woman stealing him. And he's easy to find in the dark. But if you want action, try begging, bribing, nagging, and leaving! And in that order.

"Holding My Nose" drew this communique from a literary buff:

DEAR ABBY: The wife who said her husband smelled because he seldom bathes reminds me of a story they tell about Samuel Johnson, the noted English lexicographer of the 1700s.

Johnson was a "purist" where words were concerned, but when it came to his personal hygiene, he was a notorious slob.

A woman passenger sitting next to him on a coach train said: "Sir, you smell!" Whereupon Johnson replied: "Madam, you are wrong. You smell, I stink."

Perhaps the husband who was accused of "smelling" would like to show this to his wife.

SEATTLE

Occasionally women stink too, according to "New Husband":

DEAR ABBY: I have been married for exactly one month: The other night I discovered that my wife uses mayonnaise on her hair before she goes to bed. She has the preposterous idea that it makes her hair grow faster. She claims that lots of women use it.

Abby, please help me as I don't care to smell mayonnaise all night.

NEW HUSBAND

DEAR NEW: There are hair conditioners on the market that are more effective and smell better. Tell your wife that when you go to bed with a tomato, you prefer to do it without the mayonnaise.

— ♥ —

Now here's a lady with a problem that some women would love to have: too much of a good thing.

DEAR ABBY: I've been married for five months to a fifty-eight-year-old sex fiend. If this letter makes no sense, it's because I no longer know what a decent night's sleep is. This man is an absolute machine. His demands are exhausting! I've told him that I neither need nor want all that sex, but he doesn't listen to me.

I have many interests. I snorkel, paint, and am interested in underwater photography, the local aquarium, Hawaiian music, and island flowers.

My husband resents my activities. All he wants is me— in bed. And I mean for hours, day and night!

How do I slow this man down?

EXHAUSTED IN HONOLULU

I advised "Exhausted" to tell her husband to see a doctor to slow him down or find a woman who was more his speed. Offers galore poured in from sex-starved women. Some were right in her neighborhood:

DEAR ABBY: I live in Waipahu, Hawaii, and I would certainly appreciate a man with drive.

My husband of thirty-seven years doesn't believe in romantic buildups, candlelight dinners, or wine. Just "Boom!" (And his "booms" came about as often as world wars!)

Just tell "Exhausted" to put her husband in a car and drive down Waipahu Street and I'll be waiting for him along with my two little ones—one kid from each world war!

WAITING IN WAIPAHU

DEAR ABBY: Our bridge club of three tables meets every Thursday. We are between forty and seventy-five years old. We would be very happy to help "Exhausted in Honolulu" solve her problem by offering our assistance on an odd-even basis every day except Thursday, our club day.

Each of us could rotate on eight-hour shifts, or be available four days on and four days off—like firemen.

We all lead very active lives but could arrange schedules to help a sister in distress.

Bless that poor unfilfilled man. He's only fifty-eight. May he have many more happy years and die with a smile on his face.

Sign us. . .

LAKKA-LUVA-WAUNNA-MANNA

DEAR ABBY: "Exhausted in Honolulu" should be married to my husband. He's a nice-looking man, forty-nine, and he's been too tired for lovemaking for as long as I can remember. But he's not too tired to play tennis, jog, ski, and disco-dance by the hour.

"Exhausted" would love this guy. I can guarantee that

he won't bother her from one year to the next. And if her husband wants to meet a woman who wouldn't mind being bothered night and day, I'll be glad to send him plane fare. Sign me. . .

NO ACTION IN COLORADO

The big question: What's normal?

DEAR ABBY: I am forty-four and Louie is forty-nine. I work in a laundry ten hours a day, and when night time comes I need a rest. Louie still acts like a teen-ager when it comes to sex. He can't get enough.

On weekends if we go for a drive in the country, he starts looking for an abandoned farmhouse or a secluded road. When we go for a walk in the woods, he's always looking for some bushes for us to crawl under.

I got so tired of being hounded for sex, I made Louie ask our family doctor how much sex was normal for people our age. He said three times a week is normal, so now Louie keeps a record. If it's less than three times a week, he says I owe him, and he adds it to next week's quota.

I am falling behind, and dread the thought of going on a vacation trip with this man.

WORN OUT

If misery loves company, "Worn Out" should be comforted by "Pooped in Pensacola":

DEAR ABBY: I'm also worn out. I've been married for six

years now and my husband acts like we're still on our honeymoon. He can't keep his hands off me. We can have sex for an hour straight and in fifteen minutes he's ready to go again. Is that normal? Help!

POOPED IN PENSACOLA

My mail has turned up a number of women who don't object to mattress acrobatics—it's the timing that bothers them:

DEAR ABBY: My problem is a very loving husband. That's the trouble. He's too loving. For example, this morning he drove the kids to school and came back thinking I'd drop everything and make the bedroom scene with him.

Will you please tell him that the time for romance is after all the kids are asleep?

Also, he always gets ideas after bowling. Bowling wipes me out, but for him it's an afrodeeshiak (or however you spell it). I wouldn't mind if I could sleep the next morning, but I have to get up to drive the carpool. Am I wrong to complain? We're not newlyweds. We've been married for seventeen years.

NO BRIDE

I told "No Bride" that the ideal time for romance is when both parties are in the mood, and she should shoot the ducks while they're flying.

DEAR ABBY: I am twenty-two and Mike is twenty-five. We've

been married a little over a year, and I have a problem I can't ask anyone else about.

Mike has a big appetite for sex, but I'm not complaining. It's his timing that bothers me. He always wants to make love on Sunday morning before mass. Abby, I know that married love is not a sin, but for some silly reason I just hate to go to mass right after having sex. Lately I have been putting my husband off. But I feel guilty about that.

Do you think I should postpone the lovemaking until after mass? Or keep telling myself I have no reason to feel guilty about it, and just try to get over that feeling. What's wrong with me?

                                    MAGGIE IN MANHATTAN

DEAR MAGGIE: Your problem is rooted in the notion that sex is sinful. You grew up believing it, and even though you're married and there is nothing to feel guilty about, you're still programmed to equate sex with sin. Talk to a priest, or a psychiatrist. (Try a priest first, it's cheaper.)

God bless "Maggie." Her letter provided me with enough column material for a week.

DEAR ABBY: Thirty years and six great kids ago, my wife, like "Maggie," was a "never-before-mass-gal." She also believed that sex was dirty and sinful.

An old priest put a stop to all that nonsense. He pulled a book from the top shelf of his library and handed it to my wife with instructions for her to call him after every chapter. He also instructed me never to let two weeks go by without bringing my wife a rose.

When the kids were little, our family doctor wrote on a prescription pad, "One weekend, every six weeks, get a sitter for the kids, buy a bottle of wine, check into a motel with your wife, and treat her like a hooker. And don't say you can't afford to. You can't afford not to."

Today our children are educated, well-adjusted and independent, and I am left with a lovable, exciting wife. Thank you, Father Joe and Doctor Bob!

CHRISTIANS SHOULD BE LOVERS

DEAR CHRISTIAN: Right on. And so should Jews, Buddhists, Moslems, Hindus, etc.

DEAR ABBY: "Maggie in Manhattan," a happily married woman, wrote to say that her husband wants to make love on Sunday morning before mass, but she feels guilty going to mass right after having sex.

Your answer, that she was still programmed to equate sex with sin, was incorrect.

To a Catholic, who knows that the marital embrace is blessed by God, your Freudian prejudices appear ludicrous in this connection. "Maggie's" guilt is obviously associated with the traditional eucharistic fast.

Until Vatican Council II, Catholics who wished to receive communion were required to abstain from eating and drinking from midnight preceding mass, though now it is reduced to one hour.

Although there is nothing immoral about food, we do not partake of it immediately preceding mass and communion. It is thus logical that "Maggie" feels she should abstain from all other pleasures, including sex.

UNDERSTANDING IN ANN ARBOR

DEAR ABBY: With regard to "Maggie in Manhattan": I went to the Irish priest of our little church some time ago and asked him the same question, "Is it all right to have sex before mass?"

With a twinkle in his eye and a lilt in his slight brogue, he answered, "I suppose it's all right if you're married and don't block the aisle."

INFORMED IN ARIZONA

Obviously the controversy about sex—too much or not enough—could go on endlessly. But the following letter brought truckloads of mail that kept my staff swamped for weeks:

DEAR ABBY: My husband has been reading up on the subject of sex, and he is of the opinion that if a woman doesn't enjoy sex right up to the grave, there must be something wrong with her.

At age fifty, and after thirty years of marriage, I would like to forget about sex altogether. Believe me, I've paid my dues.

Where is it written that a woman should be ready and willing to perform every time her man beckons? I suspect that many (if not most) women get very little physical satisfaction out of sex; they just go through the motions because they want to do something for men they love.

I can't believe that I'm the only woman who feels this way. Please poll your readers, Abby. And if they're honest, I think you will find that I am right.

TIRED IN LINCOLN, NEB.

I invited women to send me a postcard or letter stating whether they agreed or disagreed with "Tired." I told them they need not sign their names, only their ages.

When we finally tallied the survey, here were the results:

Total responses:　　　　227,606
Agreed with "Tired":　　114,005
Disagreed:　　　　　　　113,601

Didn't I tell you the bedroom blues singers were divided about equally?

Here were some sample comments:

"I'm fifty, raised two children, married twenty-nine years, cared for a semi-invalid mother, moved fourteen times, worked almost my entire married life as a nurse, and believe it or not, it's my husband who's tired!"

RICHMOND, VA.

"I always took a couple of stiff drinks to face what was waiting for me in the bedroom. I'm sixty-three and still hate sex, but I sure love booze."

BALTIMORE

"There must be something wrong with 'Tired.' I'm eighty-one, and when my husband was alive I thought sex was the most fun in the world, but now that I'm a widow, it's kind of hard to find someone to play with—especially in a small town where everyone knows your business."

HAVING FUN AT EIGHTY-ONE

"I'm fifty-one, and now that our kids are out of the house we can make love in the afternoon, make all the noise we want, and I don't have to worry about getting pregnant.

This is the best time of my life!"

HAPPY IN DENVER

"How can I enjoy sex when my husband comes to bed with his teeth out, needing a bath, and belching onions in my face? I'm fifty-five and agree with 'Tired.'"

NO NAME IN CLEVELAND

"I've been a widow for twelve years. My husband and I both enjoyed sex until he died. He was ninety. I could still enjoy it, but who would have me?"

JUNE, AGE EIGHTY-ONE

"I was told that a decent woman wasn't supposed to enjoy sex, so I felt guilty when I did. My husband died, and when I married again at forty-six, I learned how to enjoy sex without shame or guilt. Sex with the right man is wonderful."

LAURA, AGE SEVENTY-SEVEN

"I agree with 'Tired.' Even a hooker gets to retire."

TIRED IN EVANSVILLE, ILL.

" 'Tired' is out of her tree. I'm soon to be fifty, married over twenty-five years, and can't get enough of that wonderful stuff."

FOXY IN FT. WORTH

"I agree with 'Tired.' Sex is much ado about nothing. I

say, 'If you want something done right—do it yourself.'"

ALONE AND HAPPY

"I'm also tired. Tired of living with a slob. I have to nag my husband to shower and use a deodorant. I don't think he knows where his toothbrush is. So if he can live without a toothbrush, I can live without sex."

I'M FIFTY-THREE . . . HE'S FIFTY-EIGHT

"'Tired' is gonna be surprised when she finds out there's sex after death, 'cause if there isn't, how could it be heaven?"

EVY IN ST. PAUL

"We took a poll at our office. Nine women agreed with 'Tired,' and six disagreed. (Five out of those six were under thirty. What do they know?)"

THE OFFICE GANG IN CHICAGO

"I'm sixty-nine and my husband is seventy-nine, and I have been pretending for years that he satisfies me. He doesn't, but he'd be crushed if he knew, and besides, it takes less than a minute."

FIRST CLASS ACTRESS

"After thirty-five years of marriage to the same man, I equate sex with any other bodily function—like blowing one's nose. I'm with 'Tired.'"

BORED IN TEXAS

"Just before we were married (at nineteen), my mom gave me a little pep talk about sex. She said, 'Honey, sex is a man's game, and women aren't supposed to enjoy it, they are just men's playthings. So pretend you're enjoying it and put up with it to make him feel like a man.'

"I said, 'But, Mom, what if I like sex?'

"She said, 'You're just like your father!'"

ALLENTOWN, PA.

"Tell 'Tired in Lincoln, Neb.,' if she's still faking it after thirty years she can send her husband to Milwaukee. I'm sixty-two and my husband is dead, but I'm not."

WILLING IN WISCONSIN

"So 'Tired' submits to sex as a favor to her husband. Tell her, if she wants to do something 'nice' for the man she loves, to bake him a cake!"

ALASKA LADY, AGE FIFTY-SIX

"Thanks for asking for this survey. I thought I was the only fifty-year-old woman who was tired of sex. I'm also tired of cooking."

WINNIPEG, CAN.

"Would you believe after twenty-five years of marriage my husband still sets the alarm for 6 A.M. so he can have sex before breakfast? You'd better believe I am also tired!"

HOUSTON

DEAR ABBY: About your survey concerning sex: Men use affection and romance to get sex. Women use sex to get affection and romance. Count me as a fifty-five-year-old woman who is glad she no longer needs a man for any of the above. Sign me. . .

TOO SOON OLD, TOO LATE SMART

DEAR ABBY: I am not a loose woman, but anything gets boring with the same person after twenty-five years.

Where I work, there are 103 married women between nineteen and sixty-five, and just for fun, I decided to ask each woman if she had ever had an extramarital affair.

Of course I didn't expect an answer, but behold—73 said yes, 21 said they would if they thought they could get away with it, and 9 told me it was none of my business.

NOSY IN TUCSON

Then I got a letter from a member of the opposite sex:

"I'm eighty-two and my wife is eighty, and after fifty years of marriage, we still enjoy our conjugal relationship. Abby, why are you asking only the women? Please take a survey to poll the men. It will open your eyes, dearie."

SCOTTSDALE

I told "Scottsdale" thanks, but I was too "Tired" from the deluge of mail precipitated by "Tired in Lincoln, Neb."!

7

Smokey The Bore

When it comes to smoking, I'm a segregationist! And I'm delighted to report that cities by the score are currently passing antismoking laws to prohibit smoking in public places: buses, subways, theaters, museums, hospitals, etc. Perhaps the organization "S.H.A.M.E." (acronym for Society to Humiliate, Aggravate, Mortify, and Embarrass Smokers) overstates the case. But personally I appreciate signs that say, "If Smoking Is YOUR Monkey, Keep Him OFF My Back!" In recent years, my cascade of mail has told me that the public is joining the crusade against smoking.

DEAR ABBY: I surely do sympathize with the reader whose friend's smoking made him sick.

I had the same problem with my dad. He would always smoke cigars in the car. One time when I was about seven, he was smoking a cigar in the car, and I said, "Dad, your cigar is making me sick."

He replied, "No, it's not."

Then I said, "Yes, it is."
He repeated, "No, it's not."
Then I threw up in the car.
He hasn't smoked cigars in the car since.

MIKE IN CULVER CITY

I don't know what it will take to curb the universal smoking habit, short of another "noble experiment" like Prohibition, which was a disaster. It is all very well to say a fully informed smoker has the right to kill himself with cigarettes if he wants to, but how do you keep him from taking everybody else along with him? Cigarette addiction is the only habit I know in which the addict not only insists that you share his poison, but gets pretty huffy about it if you object.

Although I have never smoked, in past years I would meekly tolerate it when I found myself in the company of those who selfishly satisfied their craving for tobacco.

Obviously they didn't realize—or didn't care—that they were forcing others to accept the indignity of breathing their fumes and smoky exhalations.

In recent years, however, I've become a bit bolder, and if I'm asked, "Do you mind if I smoke?" I politely reply, "Not if you don't mind if I choke."

A reader, bless him, asked me why I thought people smoked. And boy, was I glad he did:

DEAR ABBY: My wife said she saw a grown woman walking down the street with a pacifier in her mouth! I said she must have been trying to quit smoking, otherwise she'd feel too silly to go out in public that way.

My wife and I were both heavy smokers, but we recently gave it up because we wanted to experience the joy of breathing through clean lungs again and rediscover our senses of taste and smell.

I said I could understand that woman's walking around with a pacifier in her mouth. She was replacing one bad habit with one that was less damaging.

Abby, why do you think people smoke? Is it a nervous habit? Is it an infantile compulsion of smokers to have something in their mouths to comfort them? Or is it simply an unconscious death wish?

QUIT IN CLARKSBURG

DEAR QUIT: Most young people begin to smoke because they think it makes them look "grown up" or smart, or to emulate someone they admire. Some smoke to keep another smoker company. They continue to smoke because they "enjoy" the feeling of relaxation it gives them (at first), and many say it keeps their weight down. Then they become addicted. (Nicotine is habit-forming, and don't let anyone tell you it isn't.) The "unconscious-death-wish theory" is also valid. Anyone who persists in doing that which he knows could be his undoing is unconsciously hastening his end.

— ♥ —

No need to review the well-publicized fact that smoking can be hazardous to one's health. Everybody knows that. My mail indicates that it can also be hazardous to one's *marriage*:

DEAR ABBY: My husband has always been a heavy smoker. (Four packs a day for the last thirty years.) Al had a heart attack last year, and the doctor gave him some orders. Quit smoking (which he did, believe it or not) and avoid all excitement. (He was more specific: absolutely no fooling around with young girls unless he wanted to die in bed.)

Now Al tells me he's nervous and restless. He says he has to lead a more "normal" life and can't give up anything he enjoys. He's asked me if I would rather have him go back to smoking again or fooling around with young girls. Isn't that a choice for you?

How should I answer him? With all his faults, I do love him and don't want to be a widow. But which is worse, lung cancer or a heart attack?

AL'S WIFE

DEAR WIFE: It's a draw. But with a choice like that, you'd probably worry less if you saw Al smoking. (P.S. Your Al certainly is a shrewd trader.)

— ♥ —

DEAR ABBY: Every time a letter appears in your column from someone who hates cigarettes, and puts down cigarette smokers, my husband accuses me of writing it. You had such a letter in your column recently and since I got the "credit" for writing it, even though I didn't, I am now putting in my two cents' worth.

I'll put it in the form of a "Dear Abby" letter:

DEAR ABBY: If all your lovely new furniture already has cigarette burns in it, and your husband always smells as if he's been fighting a fire in a tobacco warehouse, and the smell of stale tobacco on his breath kills all inspiration for romance, are those sufficient grounds for divorce?

My husband's kisses taste terrible. He is a very affectionate man, and he knows how I feel about his smoking because I have told him that that is the reason for my holding out in the romance department, so why in Heaven's name does he continue to smoke?

HOLDING OUT

DEAR HOLDING OUT: Because your husband, poor slave, is "hooked" and thus far has been unable to kick the habit. But I don't recommend the "hold out" technique. He might turn to something (or someone) else.

DEAR ABBY: My husband is fifty-five, and thank God he's in pretty good health, but every time he hears that someone he knows under seventy-five dropped dead, he announces that he is going to "start living." Abby, Harry has been "living" all his life, and if he has ever missed anything, I don't know what it could be.

Well, Harry started "living" again after he buried a fifty-seven-year-old friend. Not only is he eating all the things he shouldn't, but he's started to smoke again—which is strictly against his doctor's orders.

Abby, he quit two years ago, and he was telling everybody how much better he felt.

Now he says he is not going to deny himself anything because tomorrow his number might come up.

So what is a wife supposed to do with a husband like that? I love him.

HARRY'S WIFE

I told Harry's wife to hit him over the head with his life insurance policy and if he didn't get the message, to nag him.

DEAR ABBY: My husband (I'll call him "Ray") spent six weeks in the hospital with a coronary and emphysema, but thank God he is going to be all right. His doctor told him he had to lose forty-five pounds and give up cigarettes. Ray lost twenty-six pounds in the hospital and he didn't have one cigarette, which isn't easy for a three-pack-a-day man.

When I was at the hospital to take Ray home, his doctor walked into his room smoking a cigarette! Ray kiddingly asked the doctor for a cigarette, and would you believe, the doctor gave him one! (I could have strangled that doctor!)

Ray has been home for three weeks and he's smoking again. I just know if that doctor hadn't given him a cigarette, Ray would have quit for good.

When I told the doctor what I thought of him, he said, "I didn't think one would hurt him. Besides, I know how much he wanted one, because I can't quit either."

What do you think of that, Abby? If I hadn't witnessed this I never would have believed it.

                                                    DISGUSTED

DEAR DISGUSTED: So what else is new? That doctor used inexcusably poor judgment, but if all the doctors who are hooked on nicotine were laid end to end, they would reach the Sloane Kettering Institute—which isn't a bad idea.

Face it, most people are too timid to speak up and renounce the rascal who fouls the air. So in preference to a direct confrontation, the next best thing is to write to Dear Abby and hope she prints the letter. These readers did:

DEAR ABBY: I have written a letter to a very dear friend of mine, and my problem is I haven't the courage to send it. If you publish it, I am sure my friend will see it. Here it is:

My dear, dear friend:

How else can I say it? You make me sick! No matter how I try to avoid the smoke of your cigarette, it's there, irritating my eyes and my sinuses and getting into my lungs.

After a few hours with you, I'm literally ill. Sometimes when you blow your smoke directly at me, I turn my head or try to "fan" it away with my hand. You offer a small apology and move your cigarette—but you never put it out!

Of course, my problem is that I am a coward. I like you too much to tell you to your face that you are selfish. I don't want to hurt your feelings, yet you go on hurting mine.

Do you know that your breath is always bad? And no amount of perfume can mask the smell of stale smoke that's constantly on your hands, clothing, and hair.

I love your company. Your sense of humor is priceless, and you've demonstrated your friendship to me many times. Yet, my doctor has told me I must avoid you. Can you believe that? Your smoking is making me ill. I miss you.

SMOKED OUT

DEAR ABBY: I am a schoolteacher with a serious bronchial condition. The doctor told me I should not even be where others are smoking. Well, I put a sign up in my apartment reading, "Thanks for not smoking."

Everyone who has come to visit me has respected that request, and I really appreciated it. Last week I had a few guests who had never visited me before. When one of them saw the sign, she said: "Don't think I am staying here and not smoking. Give me an ashtray!"

When I told her I didn't have any ashtrays she asked for a dish. I refused. I served coffee, and she and the others smoked and used their cups for ashtrays.

Abby, I couldn't believe it. I didn't want to hurt them, but I hurt myself. That night I couldn't sleep, and the next day I couldn't use my voice to speak to my students.

Please print this. I know they read your column. It might help. Sign this. . .

OFF MY CHEST

DEAR ABBY: I cannot tolerate smoke, but it seems the world is geared for smokers. In waiting rooms and in almost all public places. If the nonsmoker wants to escape the pollution of smokers, he has to find a smoke-free corner where he can breathe some fresh air.

Why don't they post NO SMOKING signs in all places where people gather, and provide the smokers with a dinky, little airtight room off to one side somewhere where they can all crowd in together, smoke to their hearts' content, and inhale each others' smoke? Then, the fresh air will be left for those of us who are more deserving of it.

SMOKE SICK

DEAR ABBY: Boy, O, boy, have I got some news for you. My beds aren't made and my dishes are still in the sink, but I've got to get this into the mail. All your talk about smoking and lung cancer won't mean a thing to people who smoke. They'll go right on smoking because they're hooked. And kids will start, too, because they see grown-ups do it, and they think it's smart. And they'll soon be hooked, too.

But, maybe this will make some of those smokers sit up and take notice. They stink! Yes, every cigarette smoker has a terrible odor about his breath, his hair, his skin, and his clothes. Why, even their hands stink! All the money they spend on perfumes and breath-deodorants is wasted.

You can still smell a smoker three feet away. If you don't believe me, the next time you go to kiss a child, ask him how he likes it. He'll tell you the truth.

Very truly yours,
Ex-Smoker

DEAR ABBY: The young married woman across the hall from me accepted $500 from her father-in-law for having "given up" smoking. (She's pregnant.) Yet she comes over here every day to beg cigarettes off me. I like her a lot and hate to refuse her, but I don't like being a party to this sort of deception. Any suggestions?

A FRIEND

I advised this friend to cut off the tobacco supply and be prepared to see the friendship go up in smoke.

DEAR ABBY: I used to operate a small excavating business that included digging graves. Whenever I was asked, "Do you mind if I smoke?" I'd reply, "I don't smoke myself, but I encourage others to. It's good for my business."

DIGGER McTAVISH

In a weak moment, I decided to let a smoker have his say. (But I couldn't resist having the last word.)

DEAR ABBY: I resent the way people are now trying to make smokers feel like second-class citizens.

Smoking is a nervous habit, right? Well, I put up with the nervous habits of others. Some folks crack their knuckles, others clear their throats, some have nervous coughs, or they sniff. People with nervous tics also make me nervous, but I don't mention it.

So, since smoking is also a nervous habit, why can't people be as tolerant of *my* nervous habit as I am of theirs?

PIPE SMOKER

DEAR SMOKER: Because your nervous habit pollutes their air, that's why. Now put that in your pipe and smoke it!

— ♥ —

DEAR ABBY: Everybody complains about smokers, but nothing is ever done about them. I've had more meals spoiled and more pleasant hours of socializing ruined by people who foul the air with cigarette and cigar smoke. Do they think they own the world? I wish someone would invent a "pipe" to be used in self-defense by nonsmokers who wish to retaliate. It should be an instrument capable of producing great clouds of offensive smoke that would outsmell any cigarette or cigar on the market. It should contain a safety valve so the user could send out this smoke without getting any of it in his own mouth. Also, tiny fans to direct the smoke away from the user and toward others. It should have an attachment that would blow ashes into the food of smokers and burn neat little holes in fine furniture.

If the above-described "retaliator" is ever invented, I promise to buy the first one produced, regardless of price.

DOUG

I told "Doug" that if such an item was ever produced he could buy the second. I want to buy the first!

8

Fooling Around

Wife: "How much would you charge for getting the
goods on my husband?"

Detective: "Five hundred dollars."

Wife: "Start right away. I can borrow that much from
my boyfriend."

Over one hundred years ago, Alexander Dumas, a
Frenchman who supposedly knew his women, said, "The
chain of wedlock is so heavy that it takes two to carry it—
and sometimes three."

So it should come as no surprise to learn that the practice of fooling around is probably the one activity that
provides me with more column material than any other.

If my mail is an accurate barometer, no one is too old
to fool around. I hear from men and women in their
eighties and nineties who confess sheepishly that they
have a taste for "forbidden fruit." (The advantages are
obvious. At their ages they don't have to pray for a crop
failure.)

The small fry fool around, too. They're never too young to play "doctor," even though they're not old enough to operate.

The singles fool around. Married folks fool around and those who claim they don't, write about those who do.

It's an ancient practice rooted in restlessness, boredom, or just a human hankerin' for variety. There are biblical injunctions about fooling around and civil laws prohibiting it. But, alas, it is still with us. And now, the evidence:

DEAR ABBY: Here's a switch for you: Why should a married man who is seeing another woman on the side (me) keep telling me what a wonderful lover his wife is?

If she's so wonderful, what am *I* doing in the picture?

PUZZLED

I suggested to "Puzzled" that perhaps he was trying to get her to try harder because she was number two.

— ♥ —

DEAR ABBY: My husband had too much to drink last night and confessed that the reason he bought me an expensive overnight bag for Valentine's Day was because he'd bought one for his girlfriend and he felt guilty. Now I don't even want the bag.

What do you think?

B. J.

I told "B. J." I thought her husband should quit drinking and looking at bags.

— ♥ —

I frequently hear from people who suspect their mate of "fooling around" and write to me for confirmation of the evidence:

DEAR ABBY: My husband and I have been married three years. I thought we had a good marriage, although our sex life seemed to be going downhill. (He was always too tired.)

My mother, who lives four hundred miles away, phoned to say that my father had suddenly become very ill, so I went to be with her for a week. On returning home I found a pair of earrings for pierced ears on the nightstand beside our bed!

I showed them to my husband and demanded an explanation. He swore he'd never seen them before and had no idea how they got there. What should I do?

MY SIGN IS LEO

DEAR LEO: Don't hassle him. Just keep your eyes open for a woman with two extra holes in her head.

DEAR ABBY: My husband is having an affair with a widow who lives across the street. When he drives by her house, he slows up and blinks his lights. Then she flips her Venetian blinds. They signal back and forth, then later he makes up excuses to get out of the house to meet her. He says they are only good friends, but I know that she is man-hungry and has an eye for my husband. How should I put a stop to this?

JEALOUS

DEAR JEALOUS: You can't stop a man from blinking his lights, neither can you prevent a woman from flipping her Venetian blinds. If you think he is "blinking" for her and she is "flipping" for him—get them both together and have a truth or consequence session.

DEAR ABBY: I've been married to a good-looking cross-country truck driver for ten years. I'm not the suspicious type, but Friday night he came off the road with two long scratches on his left hip. They were fairly deep scratches, yet neither his shorts nor his trousers were ripped.

When I asked him where he got the scratches, he said they were probably from a feather in the bed. Now, Abby, I'd like to believe him, but do they still have feather-bedding in modern motels? And could anybody get scratched like this from a feather?

NOT DUMB

DEAR NOT: It's unlikely that the scratches came from a feather. It was probably the whole chick.

DEAR ABBY: This morning I was going through my husband's wallet, and I came across a list of ladies' sizes for everything from coats, dresses, gloves, and hosiery to bras. It was "signed" with a lipstick imprint, "From your Honey." What does this mean?

ARLINGTON

DEAR ARLINGTON: It probably means that you can't trust your husband, and somebody else can't trust your husband's memory. (At least you know the vital statistics of your competition.)

DEAR ABBY: Last summer I found a pair of worn pantyhose under the seat of my husband's pickup. When I asked him whose they were and what they were doing there, he said they were probably mine and he uses them to clean his windshield.

I knew they weren't mine because I don't wear that kind, but I let it go to avoid a fight.

I forgot all about the incident until yesterday when I came across a pair of fancy panties in the glove compartment of his pickup. I knew for sure they weren't mine because this pair had "Friday" on them.

Now I'm really suspicious. Be a pal and print this, Abby. I want that chick who's been fooling around with my husband to know what happened to "Friday."

SUSIE IN SPOKANE

DEAR SUSIE: If your husband continues picking up in his pickup he should warn his friends to pick up after themselves. Daily—Monday through Sunday!

— ♥ —

All work and no play makes Jack a dull boy—unless, of course, Jack plays around at work. Many Jills suspect he does:

DEAR ABBY: Jack and I have had a fairly good marriage for fourteen years—until five months ago, when he started giving driving lessons after work to supplement his income.

Most people can learn to drive a car in a month, but there's this attractive divorcee he's been giving lessons to for nearly four months. Every time I ask about her, he tells me she is far from being ready to take her driver's tests, as she is a slow learner. Jack always gives this woman his last appointment, and he comes home late and dead tired.

I am suspicious. What do you think?

MILWAUKEE MRS.

DEAR MRS: It appears that your husband is "supplement-
ing" more than his income. Tell Jack that if his slow-learn-
ing client can't drive a car by now, she should get a horse
and quit horsing around with the driving instructor.

Then there are those who think fooling around is con-
vention-al behavior:

DEAR ABBY: Last winter, when my husband attended a con-
vention out of town, he got involved with a lady delegate
in her hotel room. When Alfred came home he told me
about it, which I appreciated, but instead of saying he was
sorry and would never do it again, he said he'd do it again
if he ever got the chance.

Fortunately, Alfred doesn't get many opportunities to
travel. He has always said that he would never have an
affair with a local woman because this is a small town and
he's afraid of gossip, and I believe him, but I know I'll
worry the next time he leaves town.

I asked him what he would do if I got involved with
another man and he said he'd break my neck. Is this fair?
He thinks he is being fair with me because he's telling me
in advance. What should I do?

ALFRED'S WIFE

DEAR WIFE: Tell him you are being "fair" with him, because
you are telling him in advance that if he repeats his con-
vention capers you will break his neck.

DEAR ABBY: Three years ago, my fifty-eight-year-old husband had a brief affair with his secretary. It was no secret, and all the tongues in this little town were wagging a mile a minute.

Once I found a motel key in his coat pocket, and he had the gall to tell me that he got tired driving so he checked into this motel to take a little nap. (Three miles from home!)

Well, last year he had an operation which left him practically impotent, and since then I couldn't ask for a more devoted husband. He phones me if he knows he's going to be half an hour late. He buys me presents, sends me flowers, and even takes me on business trips, which he never did before.

Of course I'm enjoying all this, but why in your opinion has my husband suddenly turned over a new leaf?

WONDERING

DEAR WONDERING: Probably because there's not much left under the old one.

— ♥ —

When Sir Walter Scott wrote about that tangled web we weave when first we practice to deceive, he must have known someone who was fooling around:

DEAR ABBY: My husband came home a little early and I didn't hear him. I was on the telephone talking to "B" at the time. ("B" is a guy I've had something going with for about a year. He's a friend of my husband's.)

My husband could tell I was talking to some guy because I hung up real fast when I saw him, so he asked me who my "boyfriend" was. I lied and told him it was "J" (another friend of his), but I told him that nothing ever happened between us. (It's true, nothing did.)

Since this incident, my husband has been very cool to "J." I feel awful and want to clear "J's" name, but I'm afraid if I do my husband might suspect "B." What should I do?

In Mess in K.C.

I told her to tell her husband that the guy on the phone wasn't "J," and if he guessed it was "B," she better run like "H."

— ♥ —

Then there was "Sylvia," the Connecticut housewife whose husband thought she was fooling around. According to "Sylvia," his suspicions were unfounded and she was willing to take desperate measures to reassure him:

DEAR ABBY: I'm twenty-eight and my husband is thirty-three. We've been married for six years, and our marriage would be ideal if it weren't for his jealousy, which is so intense it borders on insanity!

He has tried everything from psychiatry to prayer meetings, but nothing has helped.

I have never given him any cause to doubt me, but he doesn't trust me out of his sight. The only thing I can think of that would give him complete peace of mind is a chastity belt!

Will you please tell me where I can get one? I know they haven't been used since the Middle Ages, but there must be one around somewhere. Or perhaps someone who works in metals could make one for me. Whatever the price, it will be worth it.

Please rush your answer to me. This is no joke.

SYLVIA IN GREENWICH

I told "Sylvia" that the only chastity belts I had ever seen were in museums, but if I heard of a metalsmith willing to fashion one for her I'd let her know. It turned out lots of people were willing to help her iron out her problems:

DEAR ABBY: I know exactly what "Sylvia" is going through.

I've been married for fourteen years to a wonderful man whose only fault was his unreasonable jealousy. He loved me dearly, and although I've always been a true and faithful wife, he never trusted me out of his sight.

The daily accusations, denials, and fighting were destroying our marriage, so together we designed something on the order of a chastity belt.

It's a tight-fitting rubber panty girdle over which I wear an old-fashioned-type corset which laces up the back. My husband laces me into it every morning, tying the lace in a hard knot at the top where I can't reach it, let alone undo it. Over that I wear a snug-fitting wide leather belt which also fastens in the back with a small padlock like those used on suitcases. My husband carries the only key.

Every day he comes home at noon to help me in the bathroom.

This may sound like a humiliating solution, and I'm certainly not advocating it for all wives, but it saved our marriage.

HAPPY IN JULIAN, CALIF.

DEAR ABBY: We at Anvil Arms do custom work in metal. We make swords and military items for museums and personal collections. The chastity belt should be no problem at all.

Of course, it would require some redesigning, since the chastity belt was notoriously uncomfortable for the wearer. We would also need exact measurements to provide a proper fit.

J. LUTHER SOWERS, SALISBURY, N.C.

DEAR ABBY: About that woman who wanted to have a chastity belt made. A competent metalsmith should be able to make one without any problem. I don't happen to be one, but I would sure like to be at the airport when she goes through the security scanner.

PHIL McNELLIS, DETROIT

DEAR ABBY: Tell "Sylvia in Greenwich," who's looking for a chastity belt, not to be stupid.

The use of the chastity belt caused much suffering among women in medieval times.

The constant chafing of the metal against the legs caused blisters, scars and gangrenous infections. Not to mention the weight of the belt, which caused chronic backaches and serious spinal deformities.

Hopefully, we've come a long way since then. But, Abby, what would happen if the husband lost the key?

CONCERNED FEMINIST

DEAR CONCERNED: Don't worry. There's always a Yale man around when you need him.

— ♥ —

To a reader who insisted she'd want to be told if her
husband were fooling around, I said:

"I would never recommend informing a friend that his
or her spouse is having an affair.

"In the first place, it may not be true. But if it is, the
spouse possibly already knows it but is trying to put up
a good front in hopes that the fire will burn itself out.
(Some do.) Each case is different, but I still wouldn't make
it my business to inform."

Readers galore responded with their views:

DEAR ABBY: I'm glad someone finally said what I've been
thinking. If my husband were having an affair, you'd better
believe I'd want to be told. Why should I go around believing that I'm loved and satisfying his needs? If he's fooling around, I'd want to know about it so I could either get
the matter straightened out or get out while I was still
young and desirable.

At any rate, Abby, I don't go along with the outdated
philosophy of protecting the wife from the truth because
she'd be "hurt" if she found out. If she waits for her husband to tell her, she might waste half her life living in a
fool's paradise.

MIFFED IN MONTANA

"Miffed" made a valid point, but I noted that the mail
was running 3 to 1 against informing the spouse:

DEAR ABBY: Thanks for advising against telling the wife
that her husband is having an affair.

My marriage was beautiful. I was married to a man who
treated me like a queen. We had two terrific teen-aged
children. Everything was perfect until my "best friend"
told me that my husband was having an affair with a young
divorcee who was working for him. I never would have
suspected a thing if my friend hadn't opened her big mouth!

I changed from a happy, loving wife and mother to a miserable, nagging shrew. Our home, once filled with love, was filled with hostility and noisy fights.

My husband went to an early grave, a sick and sorry man, begging me to forgive him. I'm now sixty-five and alone, and regret being such a fool over something that probably would have blown over in time.

My best friend may have thought she was doing me a favor, but she ruined my life.

WITHHOLD MY NAME

DEAR ABBY: I got a telephone call from an unidentified stranger (a woman) who told me she thought I should know that my husband was having an affair with a young woman named Sheila.

My husband had indeed become infatuated with a young woman named Sheila. The affair lasted exactly four months. Then Sheila started to pressure him to divorce me and marry her. My husband then regained his senses and told her it was all over between them because he loved his family too much to break up his home.

That's when this unidentified stranger called to "tip me off." She was hoping I'd be hurt and angry and kick my husband out. Then *she* could move in for the kill. Of course, it didn't work.

STILL MARRIED

DEAR ABBY: When I was twenty (and still a virgin), I married a man who had me completely fooled. In the three and a half years that we were married, he slept with everyone he could get his hands on, including his underage cousin! No one wanted to tell me. I was, indeed, the last to know.

I will be eternally grateful to the friend who finally gathered the courage to tell me what everyone who lived in our
apartment building knew. And all the while I had been
beating my brains out trying to make a marriage work with
a husband who had been lying and cheating from the day
we were married.

Today I am divorced and a thousand times happier. And
I'm still young enough to meet someone decent and have
a good life.

GRATEFUL

DEAR ABBY: Several years ago, I took it upon myself to tell
a very close friend of mine that her husband was having
an affair with a girl in his office. I honestly thought I was
doing her a favor.

Do you know what she said to me? "Why don't you mind
your own business?"

LEARNED A LESSON IN TIFFIN, OHIO

DEAR ABBY: I'm glad you advised against telling a friend
that her husband is having an affair. Why? Because if an
affair is really going on, unless the wife is a complete idiot,
she doesn't have to be told! All the signs are there for her
to read: Suddenly he has a lot of extra "work" to do. He
starts coming home very late and very tired. Often he isn't
where he says he'll be.

A wife who has had a good marriage can tell from the
way her husband looks at her (or doesn't look at her). By
the way he touches her (or doesn't touch her). His ardor
slowly cools. ("Sorry, dear, I have a lot on my mind these
days.")

If a woman pretends she doesn't "know" when her husband is having an affair, she just doesn't want to know, which is also her right, right?

"KNEW" IN BRIDGEPORT, CONN.

Of course, fooling around can lead to divorce and re-marriage. The trouble is, the new spouse has already got your number. I'll let one such reader write the epilogue to this story:

DEAR ABBY: How about a letter from a "winner"? My mar-ried lover left his wife for me!

I was told that I wasn't breaking up anything; his mar-riage was dead long before he even met me. His wife had gotten fat. I was married too, but I assured him that my marriage was also over—my husband had gotten dull and boring.

So I divorced my boring husband and he divorced his chubby wife. Oh, yes, we both had children, but we ex-plained that we were in love and when they were older they would understand.

Our marriage was a dream come true. No more lying and sneaking around. At long last we were legally man and wife for all the world to see.

Our apartment was filled with modern funiture and old-fashioned guilt. And plenty of doubt and mistrust.

Two years later he was meeting someone new. I told him he was a liar and a cheat. He said it took one to know one.

And by the way, he's gotten a little dull and boring, and I've put on a little weight.

A WINNER

The Animal People

If you define an "animal lover" as someone who likes animals better than people, then I am no animal lover. Don't get me wrong, I really do like some animals—but not in my bed or at my table.

However, there are millions of people who prefer the company of animals to people, which is understandable, because animals are far less demanding, never ask any questions, and are easier to love.

"Animal people" not only adore animals, they "humanize" them in the way they can't bring themselves to do for their fellow human beings. A true animal lover can agonize more over a lost Chihauhua than an earthquake in Guatemala.

Of course, problems are bound to arise when a wife shows more concern for her pet than her spouse.

DEAR ABBY: I've been unhappily married for twelve years. Many times I started to get a divorce but Shapiro talked me out of it. My wife has three sisters, and all she does is travel around the country to see them. We have no children but we have two dogs, and I have to stay home and take care of the dogs because my wife refuses to leave them in a kennel. She's gone now and I'm burned up because I'd like to go somewhere myself and I can't go because of these dogs. What is your advice?

HAROLD

I told "Harold" to take the dogs over to Shapiro's and have a good time.

— ♥ —

"Animal People" will have no difficulty relating to this exchange:

DEAR ABBY: Do you believe that dogs can understand human language? My sister, Carol, insists that her poodle can.

Carol went on a three-week vacation and left "Pisher" in a kennel. When she returned she said Pisher was so furious that he wouldn't look her in the face for five days. Carol took the dog in her arms, and he turned his head away. Then she said, "If I promise never to put you in a kennel again, will you forgive me?"

She claims the poodle looked at her and nodded his head as if to say, "Yes, I forgive you." Then he nuzzled her and licked her hand.

Can you believe this? Or do you think my sister is a nut?

KAY

I told "Kay" when it comes to dog lovers, I can believe anything.

— ♥ —

Some folks carry their love for their pets a bit far:

DEAR ABBY: I saw a picture of a beautiful bride in the Sunday *Indianapolis Star*. She had been married the previous Sunday in the St. Stephen's Episcopal Church.

In the last line, describing the wedding ceremony, was the following: "The bride's pet dog, a toy Pomeranian, served as one of her attendants."

How about that?

HORRIFIED HOOSIER

DEAR HORRIFIED: It's a wise girl who knows who her best friend is.

It's always a joy to hear from young animal and bird lovers. Take these teen-age sisters who had a message for the world and chose the "Dear Abby" column to get it across:

DEAR ABBY: Here in Iowa the winters are pretty cold, so my sisters and I (we're all in our teens) have made a habit of putting out food for the squirrels, birds, and rabbits.

Today, we saw a squirrel who had been in our neighborhood for as long as we can remember. He came to eat out of a neighbor's bird feeder. Abby, this neighbor saw him, got a shotgun, and killed that hungry little squirrel while he was eating! It just made us sick.

Please print this and tell people if they don't want animals in their yard to just chase them away. You can't teach a dead animal anything.

Sign us. . .

THREE SISTERS IN WATERLOO, IOWA

Naturally, I had some kind words for the young animal lovers, but I never dreamed that my kudos to the kids who loved squirrels would earn the ire of some readers who knew more about squirrels than I did:

DEAR ABBY: For your information, squirrels belong to the rodent family and they do far more damage than rats! Squirrels not only dig around gardens, destroying plants and roots, they chase away lovely songbirds and steal their food. Worse yet, they chew and destroy telephone cable, costing phone companies millions of dollars annually. Furthermore, squirrels keep filthy nests.

I can't think of one single constructive thing those little imps do. We should have a national program to eradicate squirrels. You can't teach a squirrel anything! Period.

HATES SQUIRRELS

DEAR ABBY: I am not for killing anything except in self-defense, but squirrels can be a real nuisance.

I once had a fairly tame squirrel come into my yard regularly to get sunflower seeds from my birdfeeder. That naughty squirrel damaged my expensive new feeder with his sharp teeth and claws. At first I was very angry. Then I realized he was probably so hungry he just had to get at those sunflower seeds somehow.

I didn't shoot him, but I did put Vaseline on the pole so he couldn't climb up to the feeder.

LOVES ANIMALS

— ♥ —

No sooner did I recover from the squirrel controversy

than I received a letter which necessitated a telephone call
to my animal consultant in Palm Springs.

DEAR ABBY: Do you know anything about jaguars? We just
got one for a pet and he is a very lovable cat. We wanted
to mate him, so we borrowed a female jaguar for that pur-
pose. We put them together but he wouldn't have a thing
to do with her. She didn't seem to have any interest in him,
either, but I think if he had romanced her a little, she might
have cooperated.

My wife says she thinks our cat is homosexual. Abby,
have you ever heard of a gay cat? I asked our vet, and he
just laughed. I'd really like to know.

KEN IN FORT LAUDERDALE

DEAR KEN: I asked one of the finest vets in the profession
(Dr. Herman Salk of Palm Springs, California), and he
didn't laugh. Instead he told me that unless the female is
"in heat," the male will have nothing to do with her. And
she couldn't care less about him as well. Also, some cats
refuse to breed in captivity. Dr. Salk concluded by saying
that he had never heard of a four-legged gay cat.

— ♥ —

Well, I was willing to take Dr. Salk's word for it. But a
reader in Macon, Ga., wasn't:

DEAR ABBY: I have news for Dr. Salk, who states there are
no homosexual cats.

We have a male dog (name withheld) and a male cat
(name also withheld) who have no sex lives other than their
gay lives together. We, and our family, and what friends
we have left, can attest to this after many years of embarrassed observations.

I would make a film of these two consenting adult animals for you and Dr. Salk, but the Georgia pornography laws are too stiff.

ASHAMED IN MACON

And then there's the perennial problem of the unwelcome pet. I receive at least one hundred letters a week bearing that theme:

DEAR ABBY: If a person wants to visit you, and she knows that her dog doesn't get along with your dog, shouldn't she leave her dog home?

Frisky (my dog) and Gertrude (my friend's dog) nearly had a bloody battle once at my place because they hate the sight of each other, so my friend called up and said she was bringing Gertrude over so I should lock up Frisky. Well, I did, but Frisky knew they were here, and he cried and carried on the whole time.

I told my friend that next time she wants to visit me, she should leave Gertrude home. My friend says that since she is the guest and I am the hostess, I should defer to her wishes. How would you handle this? I really like my friend, but I don't care for her dog.

FRISKY'S MISTRESS

DEAR MISTRESS: The next time your friend wants to get together, tell her to stay home and lock up Gertrude, because you are coming to visit her and you are bringing Frisky.

DEAR ABBY: My sister and her husband have two obnoxious dachshunds.

I once jokingly hinted, "I can tie our children outside if they get on your dogs' nerves." (No reaction.) These dogs have growled and snapped at our children without provocation, and our little ones are terrified of them.

On their last visit, one of the dogs lifted his leg on my collection of African violets and all my sister said was, "Whoops, Adolph had an accident!" (It was no accident. It was deliberate.)

I like animals but these dogs are more than I can take.

DOG PROBLEM

Perhaps I should point out that cats are an exception to the universal love that "animal people" lavish on anything equipped with fur, feathers, or scales. There are some people who just can't stand cats. Others have a neurotic fear of them. Cat-lovers, though, make up for it with a regard for their feline friends which is often downright fanatical. They overcompensate. And anybody who doubts there are millions of pampered pussycats has only to count the cat-food commercials—in themselves something of a sermon in a hungry world.

DEAR ABBY: I moved into this apartment building thirty years ago. On my floor was a terminal cancer patient who had a nine-year-old cat named "Miss Chee Chee." I told her I would care for her cat after she was gone and not to worry. She left her entire "estate" to me to care for Miss Chee Chee. (It was $25.)

Well, for four days after that lady died, Miss Chee Chee wouldn't eat a thing. I bought the finest cat food I could find but she wouldn't go near it. I feared she would die, so I called a vet to find out how to get Miss Chee Chee to eat.

On the fifth day, when I had dinner on my table, my phone rang. It was my vet with more "tricks" on how to get the cat to eat. When I got back to the table, my steak, gravy, potatoes, and green beans had disappeared!

Miss Chee Chee lived for five more years, then she put her paws around my neck, gave me a hug, and died.

G. C. IN N.Y.C.

Poor Miss Chee Chee must have been on her ninth life.

Then there was a swinging cat who had a tale of his own:

DEAR ABBY: We had a cat named Maysheh who was a real swinging bachelor, and before we realized it, Maysheh had picked up ringworm and had given it to all the kids in the family. The kids had to have their heads shaved, salve was applied daily, and they had to wear caps night and day. Believe me, it was a mess.

Cats are naturally clean animals, but if a family wants to keep a cat as a house pet, it should never be allowed to cat around. Poor Maysheh was neutered at the peak of his prime and he still acts as if he's mad because he knows what he's missing.

CAT LOVER

I never thought I'd see the day when I would have to apologize publicly for saying that goats smelled bad and pigs and hogs were greedy.

First, in referring to a husband who seldom showered, I said, "No woman wants to make love to a man who smells like a mountain goat."

I should have left it at that, but I added: "And if there's an International Brotherhood of Mountain Goats, I hereby offer them my most humble apologies."

Would you believe I heard from Steve Frazee of Salida, Colorado, informing me that there was indeed an *International Order of Rocky Mountain Goats!*

He further informed me that women cannot join this organization otherwise he would gladly submit my name for membership.

I thanked Mr. Frazee, adding that I doubted if many women would care to butt into the International Order of Rocky Mountain Goats, but if they did they should not be denied membership because of their sex—and not to be surprised if he heard from the Women's Liberation Movement.

Now about the pigs and hogs: I simply said, "The person who comes into your company and hogs all the conversation is no less a pig than the person who comes to the table and eats all the food." Fair enough?

Not according to an Alabama reader:

DEAR ABBY: You besmirched the image of pigs and hogs when you implied that pigs and hogs are greedy. They are not! If these little four-footed creatures were fed balanced rations, they would not overeat! That point has been proven through research at many universities.

It's a fact that most affluent people eat themselves out of shape. So why downgrade pigs and hogs when people, who are supposed to be more intelligent than pigs, are guilty of the same thing?

If you want to emphasize greediness in people, instead

of calling them "hoggish," why not say "peoplish"?

G.B.P. IN ALABAMA

DEAR G.B.P.: I plead guilty to perpetuating the prejudicial notion that pigs and hogs are greedy. And I hope that every pig and hog who reads this will forgive me.

The pros and cons of hunting have been a lively topic in my column for twenty-five years. And it's not resolved yet:

DEAR ABBY: Last week my husband and I had a guest for dinner. My husband loves to hunt, so we served venison, which our guest said was delicious—until she heard it was deer meat. Then she flew into a rage! She went on and on about how cruel and inhuman it was to kill defenseless animals just for the sport of it. She said people who destroyed wildlife were sick and depraved!

We were stunned. My husband tried to explain that wildlife cannot be stockpiled, and if hunting were outlawed, the wildlife would overpopulate and die of starvation.

She said she didn't believe a word of it—that Nature would provide.

Sign us. . .

ANIMAL LOVERS

It's useless to argue with animal lovers who insist they kill animals "for their own good" so I let my readers say it for me:

DEAR ABBY: Those hunters who kill animals so they won't overpopulate and die of starvation have got to be the biggest hypocrites of all time.

Just where do they think beef, pork and mutton come from? Anybody who's raised a 4-H calf, or nursed along a runt pig or an orphan lamb knows that these animals are every bit as lovable as the majestic buck or graceful doe.

How much kinder is death from a blow on the head with a sledgehammer than from a bullet? All meat eaters are guilty.

In case you're wondering—yes, I eat meat. And no, I don't hunt.

NO HYPOCRITE

DEAR ABBY: May I add my comment to "Animal Lovers," concerning a husband who loves to hunt:

A compassionate chaplain I once knew in the Army told me that most deer hunters were poor shots and only wounded the deer, who would then wander off to the woods to die in agony.

"My system," he explained, "is to break the deer's leg with my first shot. Then I send my dogs after him. They chase him to my car, and I shoot him there, so I don't have to carry him but can load him right on."

In short, Abby, people who love to kill will always find a way to rationalize their cruelty.

C. H. IN N.Y.C.

DEAR ABBY: One more addition to the hunting controversy: Agreed, it is cruel to only wound an animal, and no conscientious hunter would leave a wounded deer to suffer and die.

A few deer seasons back, a lady hunter in Pennsylvania managed to wound a deer, but being a truly compassionate animal lover, she battered the stricken animal's skull to bits so enthusiastically that she smashed the stock of her rifle. Newspapers praised her determination to "get her deer."

TROY READER

I don't pretend to be an authority on animals, but I was able to provide a fellow Iowan with a few little-known facts about animal and bird life:

DEAR ABBY: I am a grown woman who has a couple of questions I'm ashamed to ask anyone else because they might think I'm a moron.

1) What is the difference between a mule, a jackass and a donkey?

2) Also, does a rooster have a male organ?

EVIE IN DES MOINES

DEAR EVIE: A mule is the offspring of a male ass and a female mare. In cases where the she-ass mates with a stallion horse, the offspring is known as a "hinny"—(which is a horse on me). The mule is always sterile, but the hinny is capable of reproducing. An ass is simply a donkey. A jackass is a male donkey.

Concerning roosters: Yes, a rooster does have a male organ, but it is so small it is practically invisible. I suppose a hen would tell you it's adequate for her needs, but by human standards, it is certainly nothing to crow about!

We've heard it from the dog people, cat people, defenders of the hog, the goat, and our wildlife. Now, let's hear it for *my* favorite animal, the ape:

> DEAR ABBY: Because you have always been a good friend of the Como Park Zoo, I am asking a favor of you.
>
> We have a five-month-old female orangutan named Joy who has been invited to the Los Angeles Zoo on a "breeding loan." They have a male orangutan named Guy whom they would like to mate with Joy.
>
> Do you know anyone with an air-conditioned automobile who would be willing to drive Joy and her foster parents to Chicago to board an airplane to transport Joy to L.A.?
>
> Joy is small enough to be held in one's arms, she has good manners, and she would do no damage to the automobile.
>
> JOHN FLETCHER, DIRECTOR
> ST. PAUL COMO PARK ZOO

I told Mr. Fletcher that I would provide Joy with air-conditioned transportation to her rendezvous, hoping she returned heir-conditioned. The story has a happy ending. Joy met Guy at the Griffith Park Zoo in Los Angeles. It was love at first sight and now my husband is a monkey's uncle.

10

Paging the Aging

We are an aging nation. Every day five thousand Americans celebrate their sixty-fifth birthday. By the close of this century, one out of every eight persons will be sixty-five or older.

Thus, one of our major concerns has become the problems of our elderly: forced retirement, the inadequacy of Social Security, inflation, personal safety in a riotous and crime-ridden society, and fear of an uncertain future, to name a few.

In an effort to learn firsthand about the problems that plagued the elderly, I ran the following "Confidential" in my column:

CONFIDENTIAL TO SENIOR CITIZENS: PLEASE SEND ME A POST-CARD AND TELL ME WHAT YOUR BIGGEST PROBLEMS ARE. MONEY? HEALTH? LONELINESS? BOREDOM? AND IF YOU'VE LEARNED TO HANDLE THEM, TELL ME HOW YOU DID IT.

The response was unbelievable! Not only postcards but

letters (some of them ten and twelve pages long!) poured in. My office gave up counting after one hundred thousand.

My readers expressed gratitude for the opportunity to be heard.

"How wonderful that someone is really interested in hearing what the older person has to say. With all the emphasis on youth these days, we survivors (please Abby, not Senior Citizens!) have been made to feel useless, like so much dead timber."

More surprising was the number of older people who wrote to tell me not only the problems they faced in recent years, but how they've learned to handle them:

DEAR ABBY: Just had my seventy-fifth birthday and never felt better in my life. I walk a mile a day, stay away from boring old people, desserts, and redheaded women. I enjoy a little nip every evening before dinner but never touch a drop before noon no matter who's celebrating what.

VINCE

DEAR ABBY: I am sixty-seven years old, and I am crazy. I got this way taking care of my mother, who is ninety-two. She is the most impossible woman who ever lived. Unfortunately, she is in better health than I am. I'd sign this, but she'd kill me.

STUCK IN ENCINO

DEAR ABBY: I'm a widow, sixty-five, nice figure, and I'm told I'm attractive. My problem is finding a good man. They either drink too much and want sex, or they're too old. One older man wanted to marry me. He said: "You buy the house, Honey, and I'll cut the grass." He could hardly walk two blocks, so I'm wondering how he could cut the grass.

WINTER PARK, FLA.

DEAR ABBY: We are both seventy-seven years old, and have been married fifty-three years. First we liked each other, then we loved each other, and now we adore each other. Our problem? We would like to die together.

H AND H IN BERKELEY

DEAR ABBY: I'm a widower. Never mind my age. I live alone in a five-room house. All I want is company and someone to help me keep this place clean. No hanky panky. She would have a private room and her own TV. If she can't cook, I can. If she is under fifty-five years of age, tell her to forget it.

PAPPY IN PITTSBURGH

DEAR ABBY: I can't speak for the men, but the biggest problem most women my age have is a retired husband. Mine follows me around the house all day "supervising" the housekeeping and cooking. He has nothing to do, and he's driving me crazy. I have no privacy. Can't even talk on the phone without him listening in. I can't sign my name, and I'll have to carry this letter around in my purse until I can sneak it into the mailbox.

TRAPPED IN FORT MYERS

DEAR ABBY: I am a widow, living alone on a pension. I have arthritis, diabetes, high blood pressure, and dizzy spells.

My problem is that I have birds nesting in my drainpipe.

IRMA

DEAR ABBY: My problem is controlling my anger when people refer to me as a "Senior Citizen." Whoever thought up that ridiculous label? I am eighty-nine, keep my aches and pains to myself, take an interest in my home, church, and community, and do what I can for the other fellow. That's all it takes to stay young.

HAPPY IN SUN CITY

DEAR ABBY: I am eighty-three and have no problems. Death took my two good wives. Did not dare to try for a third. Afraid I'd get a lemon. I bowl in four leagues and enjoy church. I give better than one-tenth of my income to God because He lets me live well.

ANDY IN N.Y.

DEAR ABBY: My problem is impotence, which causes many of us men to feel humiliated, depressed, and dejected. We love our wives, but we can't perform. After the doctor completes our checkups, he smiles and says: "Sex is all in your head." That's humbug!

Here we are in Florida, the home of the Fountain of Youth, but like Ponce de Leon, we can't find the well.

READY, WILLING, BUT NOT ABLE

DEAR ABBY: I'm only a kid of ninety-two. Do I qualify for senior citizenship? I don't have any problems, but I've got a lot of relatives who are going to have plenty of problems when I die. I'm leaving everything to the church.

GRANDPA IN PHOENIX

DEAR ABBY: I'm seventy-four, wear eyeglasses, false teeth,

and a hearing aid, and I walk with a cane. But I'm happy because I'm a born-again Christian.

I can smell the fragrance of my flowers and feel the softness of my cat, and I can eat anything I can afford to buy.

I'm on an old-age pension and can't afford a radio or TV, but I have lots of good books. I can't afford a phone or even a newspaper, but I can avail myself of my neighbor's in both cases.

I've always been poor, so it's no hardship. Besides I'll have a mansion by and by.

GLADYS IN CINCINNATI

(Too bad "Gladys" didn't send along her full name and address. At least a dozen readers wrote in offering to send her a radio, TV, and even a subscription to the *Cincinnati Enquirer*. Unusual? Not at all. The generosity of my readers never ceases to amaze me. Strangers wanting to help strangers—anonymously, which is, I think, the ultimate in generosity.)

— ♥ —

Some older readers disclose that they're still young at heart:

DEAR ABBY: In a courtship between a woman sixty-five and a man sixty-seven, who should offer the first kiss?

I am a widow and he is a widower and we are getting very close to where I will need to know.

If he should make the first move, should I act coy, or should I respond? Or perhaps I should make the first move, but I don't want to push for it.

I would like a romantic relationship!

Women used to sit back and let the men make all the

overtures, but perhaps women's lib has changed all that.
Or has it?

Proper but Puzzled

Dear Puzzled: If you feel like kissing him, go ahead and
kiss him. He'll probably meet you halfway and beat you
to the finish line.

Dear Abby: I am a widow, age seventy-seven. I live in the
same apartment building with a fine gentleman with
whom I've become romantically involved. He's married
but has had a legal separation from his wife for fifteen
years. His wife won't give him a divorce without a big
settlement, which he will not agree to, as he figures he may
outlive her. (She's eighty-one and he's eighty-four.)

I'm not entirely at ease with this man, as I am afraid his
wife might sue me and I have a pretty nice savings myself.
I have heard that she still watches him very close.

He takes me out to dinner, and I have him in for meals.
We play a little gin, watch a little television, and have a
little fun. I think you get the picture, but I'm not looking
for trouble. Am I foolish?

No Name Please

Dear No Name: Ask your lawyer how much "fun" the law
allows a man in your neighbor's circumstances. I think I
get the picture, but if you aren't careful, you could get the
frame.

This man hadn't learned that eighty is enough:

DEAR ABBY: Irving and I have been married for nearly sixty years. Irving is over eighty and he's still looking. Can you beat that?

All our married lives I covered up for him because I didn't want the children to know.

Two years ago Irving moved a nice-looking younger lady into one of our rental properties. (She is about sixty-five.) I finally got so tired of having to go over there every time I wanted to find my husband, I gave her notice to vacate. Irving pouted for a long time but he finally got over it.

Now it's another woman. This one is about sixty and a real live wire. Please tell me what to do. I can't do much, as all our money is in my husband's name. No publicity, please, as I am a proud woman.

ANONYMOUS

DEAR ANONYMOUS: Be patient. It won't last forever. Nothing does.

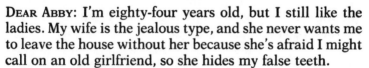

DEAR ABBY: I'm eighty-four years old, but I still like the ladies. My wife is the jealous type, and she never wants me to leave the house without her because she's afraid I might call on an old girlfriend, so she hides my false teeth.

What should I do?

GRANDPA MAX

DEAR GRANDPA: Your wife is looking out for your best interests. She wants to make sure you don't bite off more than you can chew.

— ♥ —

For some of our elders a little money is a dangerous thing:

DEAR ABBY: At age eighty-one, after having been a widower for many years, Dad married a shrewd little golddigger with dollar signs in her eyes.

After four months, Dad left her saying, "Now I don't have to die to know what hell is like."

The problem: When Dad walked out on this lady, he said, "I am sick of you. Take what you want!" (The house and everything in it was Dad's.)

Two days later when we went to the house, we nearly fainted. The place had been stripped. She had taken everything, including carpeting, draperies, fixtures, stove, and refrigerator, and she even uprooted some of the plants in the garden!

Now, Abby, you know Dad was not of sound mind when he told her to take what she wanted. What should we do? Don't suggest a lawyer. Dad is a lawyer.

TWO DAUGHTERS

DEAR DAUGHTERS: Whether Dad was of "sound mind" or not when he told the grasping little golddigger to take what she wanted, she took him literally. Dad surely knows that doctors who become ill consult other doctors, and lawyers with legal problems consult other lawyers, so he should see a lawyer. But in the meantime he'd better look for a furnished apartment.

This letter had a familiar ring to it:

DEAR ABBY: I am seventy-seven and Nick is eighty. We've been married for sixty years. Nick has always been a flashy dresser. I have a one-carat diamond ring which I don't wear any more because I am afraid of being robbed or killed. Nick said as long as I'm not wearing my diamond, he'd like to make it into a ring for himself.

Abby, it's not that I don't want him to have the diamond, it's just that I am afraid of what might happen to him.

Since I have refused him the ring, he is barely speaking to me. He also quit making love to me every Sunday afternoon which he has done for sixty years. I suppose I could live without it, but I got so accustomed to it I feel deprived.

Should I give him the ring so he will be his old sweet and loving self again?

NICK'S WIFE

DEAR WIFE: If Nick doesn't realize that you don't want him to have the ring because you are concerned about his welfare, shame on him. (P.S. Someone should tell him if he doesn't use it, he'll lose it, and I don't mean the ring.)

Now, here was a problem one could really get his teeth into:

DEAR ABBY: I am employed at a very large convalescent home. One of the elderly residents here lost her dentures, so with a pillow case in hand, she crept into the rooms of the other occupants while they were sleeping and picked up every pair of false teeth from the water glasses. She then returned to her room and tried each set until she found one that fit her. Then she sneakily returned the sets of teeth to any water glass.

The next morning, everyone was walking around the place with overbites and underslung jaws, complaining bitterly that their dentures didn't fit!

How do we straighten out this mess? Or must we buy new dentures for one hundred residents?

DENTURE DILEMMA

DEAR DILEMMA: Call in a dentist and ask him to examine the mouths of the patients and the dentures, in order to return them to their rightful owners. (P.S. Denture-marking kits are available. Get one and use it, before another teeth thief gums up the works again.)

I was speechless when a speech therapist wrote with a kind word for the denture thief!

DEAR ABBY: I say "hurray" for that little old lady who got up the gumption to replace her lost dentures, even though she had to plunder other residents of the convalescent home to do it.

I work as a speech therapist in homes for the aged, and my biggest problem is that most of these old folks refuse to wear dentures even when they have them. The result is that their faces fall in, their speech becomes thick and unintelligible and they are soon limited to mushy foods.

The poor dear probably thought she was robbed, so her philosophy was, "A tooth for a tooth."

"SPEECHIE"

I told "Speechie," "Maybe so. But 'he who takes what isn't his'n must give it back, or go to prison.'"

Like fine wine some relationships improve with age, while others grow sour:

DEAR ABBY: My husband is retired now, and most of his cronies are either dead or too sick to be any company to him. He used to be quite the "man about town" and I spent many evenings alone and heavyhearted wondering when he would come home.

Now, do you know what? I can't get him out of the house. I actually have to look for things for him to do. "Go to the grocery store! Go to the drug store! Go to the hardware store!"

I can't stand the sight of him anymore. I get nauseated when I hear his key in the door.

After he reads the morning paper, he starts to follow me around, supervising the cooking, housekeeping, etc.

If I have a friend in for a cup of tea, he moves right in and monopolizes the conversation.

Dear God, I am so sick of him, death would be a welcome release.

WEARY

DEAR WEARY: Yours or his? The quality of a marriage is only as good as the materials used by the builders. The "lumber of life" is caring, sharing, patience, forgiveness, and understanding. One can't expect to spend his twilight years in a cathedral when he's accumulated only enough "lumber" for a shack.

While reading my mail, I am often reminded of that old saying, "A mother can take care of ten children, but sometimes ten children can't take care of one mother":

DEAR ABBY: I have an elderly mother who has been in a nursing home for the last four years.

I am one of her three children (one son and two daughters). We all live within a forty-five-minute drive from the nursing home, and all of us contribute equally toward the expenses, but I am the only one who visits her. I go there every day. My brother goes once in four months. He says, "I'm sorry, I just can't take that place. It's too depressing!" Can you believe it? He'll call Mamma on the phone maybe once a week and ask her if she "needs" anything. (All she needs is for him to visit once in a while.)

My sister runs over there once a month for five minutes. She doesn't even sit down. She says the "smell" of that place makes her sick. How is that for an excuse?

Although Mamma gets confused once in a while, she is far from senile. I know she's hurt, but there's nothing I can do about it.

Please print this. The shoe will fit both a woman, size 6, and a man, size 10. Let them wear it!

                                        HAD IT IN ST. LOUIS

I told "Had It" that the shoe for this situation has no size. One size fits all.

A reader signed "Bill" asked me to define old age. I offered a light-hearted answer, based on my view that while age may be a minor inconvenience, it isn't necessarily a major handicap:

DEAR BILL: To recycle an old cliche, old age, like beauty, lies in the mind of the beholder. But I would say that you've reached it when:

You need glasses to find your glasses.

You walk into another room and wonder what you went there for.

People start telling you you're looking good, but no one says you're good looking.

You pass up a romantic encounter because you're worried about your heart.

You think today's policemen look like kids.

When Representative Claude Pepper, chairman of the U.S. House Committee on Aging, saw that column I got a blast from a hot Pepper. His letter in part:

DEAR ABBY: I am seventy-nine years young, and as an avid reader of your column I was sadly disappointed in your response to "Bill," who requested your definition of old age.

Your characterization of older people as sightless, absent-minded, ugly, and sexless is unworthy of the usual thoughtful insights your readers expect of you.

With kindest regards.
CLAUDE PEPPER, FLORIDA, CHAIRMAN,
U.S. HOUSE COMMITTEE ON AGING

Happily an Indiana gentleman came to my defense, addressing his remarks to Representative Pepper:

DEAR ABBY: I am happy to be an octogenarian myself.

Oh, come off it, Brother Pepper. Relax from the somber responsibilities of shepherding us decrepit aged and enjoy a sprightly lady columnist's light-hearted characterizations of the weight of our years without bridling.
RALPH W. SNYDER, INDIANAPOLIS

— ♥ —

Then another octogenarian put age in perspective when he wrote amusingly of the advantages of old age:

DEAR ABBY: We oldsters sure do get away with a lot just because we've managed to keep breathing longer than most folks. I have just celebrated my eightieth birthday and I've got it made.

If you forget someone's name or an appointment or what you said yesterday, just explain that you are eighty, and you will be forgiven. If you spill soup on your tie, or forget to shave half your face, or take another man's hat by mistake, or promise to mail a letter and carry it around in your pocket for two weeks, just say, "I'm eighty, you know," and nobody will say a thing.

You have a perfect alibi for everything when you're eighty. If you act silly, you're in your "second childhood."

Being eighty is much better than being seventy. At seventy people are mad at you for everything, but if you make it to eighty, you can talk back, argue, disagree, and insist on having your own way because everybody thinks you are getting a little soft in the head.

They say life begins at forty. Not true. If you ask me, life begins at eighty!

GOT IT MADE AT EIGHTY

Letters That Beget Letters

Almost every letter published in my column provokes more letters from other readers. Some write to agree with me, others to disagree, and some just want to share their experiences in a similar situation. The feedback mail ranges from helpful to hateful to hilarious.

This letter from Greenwich, Conn., on a sensitive subject, touched off a barrage of mail:

DEAR ABBY: I'm a freshman boy in high school and although I'm not Jewish, a lot of people think I am. I have a very Jewish-sounding name, and to make matters worse, I look like my father and he looks Jewish.

We live in a restricted neighborhood and belong to a country club that has no Jewish members.

I have nothing against Jews, and if I were Jewish, I would admit it, but I was baptized in the Episcopalian church. My father understands the problem, because he's had it all his life, so when I asked him if I could legally change my name when I am twenty-one, he said it was up to me. Abby, if I were to change my name do you think people would

147

think I changed it because I am really Jewish and want to hide it?

NOT JEWISH IN GREENWICH

I told "Not Jewish" that he had a right to change his name if he felt it was a handicap.

Letters poured in, among them these gems:

DEAR ABBY: The letter from the distraught Christian boy with the "Jewish-sounding" name interested me, because I'm a Christian who, because of my name, has been mistaken for a Jewess many times. But when this occurs, I feel honored, for it proves that I have done nothing to downgrade my Jewish brothers.

My first name is "Naomi" and my middle name is "Ruth." Both are Jewish names taken from the Old Testament. My maiden name is "Lehman," which could also be "Jewish" but in my case is not.

Some three thousand years ago, the biblical Ruth said, ". . . thy people shall be my people, and thy God, my God . . ." I feel indeed fortunate that, as a Christian, I have not only the gift of Christ but also the heritage of Abraham, Isaac, and Jacob. I have the kinship of David and the promises of Isaiah. I have the Jerusalem that Christ loved, and the Israel where he walked. I can join in the "song with sweet accord" that thus surrounds the throne.

Sincerely,
NAOMI RUTH LEHMAN BAULKEY

DEAR ABBY: Somebody should tell that poor jerk signed "Not Jewish" that Judaism is the cradle of Christianity, and the only difference between Christians and Jews is that the Jews are waiting for the Messiah to come, and the Christians are waiting for him to come back.

I have the opposite problem. I am Jewish, but I have a

"Christian-sounding" name, and I look like a Christian, and I have never felt that it helped me any.

Very truly yours,
ADAM J. JOHNSON

DEAR ABBY: This is for "Not Jewish" with a Jewish-sounding name, who wanted to know if he should change his name to a more Christian-sounding one.

I am an Irish Catholic woman, married to a German Lutheran with a "Jewish-sounding" name. I happen to have a very "Jewish-looking" nose, and my husband says with my nose and his name nobody would believe we're not Jewish.

I want to say that with our "Jewish-sounding" name I did not encounter as many insults as I did with my Irish-Catholic name, growing up in a Protestant neighborhood.

"NOT JEWISH" ALSO

DEAR ABBY: May I say a few words to "Not Jewish": If you are a Christian who doesn't want to be mistaken for a Jew, I have some advice for you:

Change your name to something typically Christian—like "Christiansen."

Then go to a top-notch plastic surgeon (who will probably be Jewish) and let him give you a more Christian-looking face.

Then consult one of the finest psychiatrists in your community (who will also probably be Jewish) and ask him why, when you insist you have nothing against Jews, you felt all this changing was necessary.

UNITARIAN MINISTER

DEAR ABBY: What does a Jew look like? To me, Danny

Thomas looks more Jewish than Alan King.

                                                                      D.G.

DEAR ABBY: George M. Cohan, a famous Irishman, was mistaken for a Jew occasionally because of his name. When a bigoted hotel manager refused him a room on the grounds that "we don't allow Jews," Cohan remarked, "I thought you were a gentleman and you thought I was a Jew. We were both mistaken."

                                                        PHILADELPHIA DENTIST

DEAR ABBY: I am not Jewish, but I wish I were. You see, my best friend is a Jew. He loved me so much that he died for me. His name was Jesus.

                                                           A TRUE CHRISTIAN

A reader wrote to ask why American Indians never lost their hair. Since I couldn't recall ever having seen a bald-headed Indian, I asked my readers to please send me a picture of one—if indeed one existed. Needless to say, I received pictures of enough bald and balding Indians to populate a reservation.

DEAR ABBY: Well, you asked for it. I am enclosing a picture of a bald Indian. My husband. He is "Chief Deon"—a full-blooded Sioux, born on a reservation in Pine Ridge, S.D., in 1899. He claims he lost his hair because he put too much bear grease on it when he was young.

                                              MRS. R. P. DEON, OGDEN, UTAH

DEAR ABBY: Well, you can stop your search for bald Indians. There aren't any. Where I was raised there were more Indians than whites, and I can't recall ever seeing a bald Indian. It's just characteristic of their race. Nobody ever saw an Indian with hair on his chest either.

A WHITE FROM WALLA-WALLA

DEAR ABBY: I have no picture to send you, but I give you my word that I have seen a bald-headed Indian. He was a full-blooded Choctaw from Oklahoma. We met at Alcatraz many years ago when he was doing life plus ninety-nine years. At that time he was only twenty-seven years old, and he was bald!

CHARLIE IN JACKSONVILLE

DEAR ABBY: I hear you're looking for bald Indians. Well, Sam Churchill up in Yakima, Wash., did a little research for you.

According to him, Indian Agency Superintendent Bill Schlick says he has never seen a bald Indian and he has dealt with thousands of Indians, including Colville and Warm Springs tribe members. Bill's secretary, Ethel Mae Chase, reported on the Klamath Indians in northern California and Oregon—no baldies there. Schlick's assistant, Barney Dunn, backs up both Bill and Ethel Mae. Dunn (part Sioux himself) is getting a little thin on top, but says that's because he's short on Indian blood. If I round up any more information, I will write.

YOUR YAKIMA CORRESPONDENT

DEAR CORRESPONDENT: Better yet, send smoke signals!

CONFIDENTIAL TO BIG CHIEF NO BULL: Thanks for the picture. That's funny. You don't look Indian!

DEAR ABBY: Well, you asked for it! I am a Chickasaw Indian and bald as an onion, and have been since I was in my late twenties. I don't know why I lost my hair. I never curled it, dyed it, bleached it, or sprayed it. I just washed it, brushed it, combed it, and watched it go.

If you will find something that will make it grow back, I will pay you cash, and you can name your own price. I won't be choosey about color either. Hair is hair.

LEONARD BROWN, OKLAHOMA CITY

DEAR ABBY: Your search for bald Indians was highly entertaining and I congratulate you for having come up with some interesting facts about the American Indians. Here are a few more:

The average weekly wage of the black man in Watts is roughly twice what the red man earns.

Fifty percent of all Indian children drop out of school before high school.

The infant death rate is 12 percent higher among American Indians than the national average.

The Indian suicide percentage is the highest in the United States.

The average Indian is dead at age forty-three.

Maybe that's why you rarely see any bald Indians.

Very truly yours,
VIRGINIA

Well, there you have it. Are there really fewer baldies

among the Indians? I still have reservations about that, but "Ed in East Illinois" raises another question concerning the American Indian male. Is it true that he's a better lover than the white man?

DEAR ABBY: I am a thirty-five-year-old man who's in love with a beautiful, twenty-eight-year-old divorcee. I want to marry her, but she keeps wanting more time to think it over.

In the meantime, she's seeing another man, and I'm afraid he has the edge on me. You see, he's part Kickapoo Indian, and I hear Indians are superior to the white man when it comes to lovemaking: Closely guarded tribal secrets on how to satisfy a woman are passed down from father to son. If there is any truth to that, I'm willing to pay whatever is necessary to find out.

Let me say that I was married for four years and I never had any complaints from my wife, but if Indians are better lovers than white men I would like to find out why.

Maybe your readers can help. Thank you.

ED IN EAST ILLINOIS

DEAR ED: I wouldn't touch your request with a ten-foot totem pole. Try the Bureau of Indian Affairs or the American Indian Movement.

A number of readers, however, responded pro and con. Perhaps I was conned by a couple of pros, but these letters made my day.

DEAR ABBY: This is for "Ed," who lost his girfriend to an American Indian because Indians were supposed to be better lovers than white men.

Ed had heard that closely guarded tribal secrets on how to please a woman were passed from father to son.

I'm an attractive divorcee living in San Francisco and teaching in a nearby university. I've had highly touted Italian lovers, black lovers, and even an Asian lover, whom I met at the Hong Kong Hilton (he was a lawyer from Wyoming). In addition to the above, while visiting Mount Rushmore I met a tall, handsome Indian from a tribe near Rapid City, S.D. He was a good lover but no *better* than the others. But he was exceptionally gentle.

No one ethnic group holds the secrets to superior lovemaking. The best lover I ever had was an American— Scotch-Irish-English—whom I met in Louisville, Kentucky, at the Kentucky Derby.

BUY AMERICAN

DEAR ABBY: The American Indian has it all over the white man when it comes to loving. Ask any squaw who is familiar with the "Apache Grip" or the "Kickapoo Twist."

MINNI HA HA

An executive (male-type) had a problem with his secretary (female-type) so he wrote to me requesting that I publish his letter. My answer was incidental. Many bosses as well as their secretaries identified with this one:

DEAR ABBY: I hope you will print this. There must be other executives who have this problem and don't know how to handle it tactfully.

Take a letter, Mrs. Brown:

You are an excellent secretary, but I wish you would leave your personal problems at home. I am not a marriage counselor or a financial adviser, and I have neither the time nor energy to listen to problems concerning your children.

When you confide your personal problems in me, although I may appear interested and sympathetic, the truth is, I am very uncomfortable and I resent using my time (and yours) on such matters.

I value your services and don't want to seem unkind, but I prefer to keep our relationship strictly impersonal and professional.

YOUR BOSS

DEAR BOSS: I don't know how many bosses share your view, but I'm sure many of their wives do. When a secretary starts crying on her boss's shoulder, she frequently ends up in his arms. The only way to discourage personal conversation (in the office and out) is to abort them at the onset.

DEAR ABBY: I am boiling! Mr. "Boss" asked you to publish an "open letter" to his secretary in which he tells her that he wishes she would keep her personal problems to herself. He says he is not a financial adviser, neither is he a marriage counselor, and he doesn't want her to waste his time (or hers) crying on his shoulder at the office. Well, I have a letter for him:

Dear Boss: In the six months I have worked for you, I know just about everything there is to know about your family situation. I really don't care if your wife is cold and that you'd divorce her in a minute if it weren't for your children. Also, I don't care if you do think I have beautiful hair, lovely eyes, great legs. Also, I do not want to join you to "relax" after office hours with a cocktail.

I don't want to discuss my private life with you, and some of the questions you ask are pretty embarrassing.

I am no "Dear Abby," so don't tell me your problems because I have no desire to become part of them.

And by the way, when I find another job that pays me what this one does, I'll give you my two-weeks' notice. Meanwhile, since you think I'm such an excellent secretary, how about a raise?

YOUR SECRETARY

The wife of a physician complained that her husband was no help at all when she was sick. Her complaint inspired like complaints from the wives of lawyers, hairdressers, electricians, plumbers, and photographers:

DEAR ABBY: Tell that doctor's wife to move over! (When she complained to her husband that she felt sick, he told her to take two aspirin and go to bed.) I am the wife of a prominent attorney, and here is my story:

Nearly two years ago when we moved cross country, the moving van was involved in a serious accident, and most of my prized antiques were destroyed. Yes, they were insured, but we haven't collected because my husband hasn't had time to follow up on the claim.

Last summer our six-year-old son was hospitalized for two weeks when his counselor at day camp slipped and spilled hot wax over 60 percent of my son's body! (That was the last time they attempted to make candles at camp.)

Although the camp admitted their liability and provided us with all the necessary forms, we have not collected for the hospitalization, medication, or plastic surgery because my husband hasn't gotten around to doing the legal work yet.

I have a scrapbook filled with newspaper articles written about my husband, but if you print this in your column, I will frame it and hang it in the bathroom!

LAWYER'S WIFE

DEAR WIFE: It's practically framed. (And so's your old man.)

DEAR ABBY: A doctor's wife said: "The shoemaker's kids always go barefoot." I know what she means.

My friends envy me because my husband is a hairdresser. They don't know that he hasn't touched my head in years. He promised to give me a cut and perm last year. I even went to his shop for it, but something went wrong with the color job he had done on one of his prized customers, and he never got around to me! I finally got so disgusted I went to the neighborhood shop and paid somebody else to do it.

People are always telling me how nice my hair looks. And then they add: "But why shouldn't it—you're married to a hairdresser." Ha, ha, and ha!

ROLLS MY OWN

DEAR ABBY: Are you ready for this? My husband is an electrician and I have a toaster that's in pieces. (He took it apart six months ago, but he hasn't had time to put it together yet.) Last Christmas he promised to fix my hair dryer, but he hasn't gotten to it yet. I've been trying to get him to put some floodlights around our house for two years, and all he's done so far is buy the lights, but they're still in their original boxes.

I give up!

ELECTRICIAN'S WIFE

DEAR ABBY: I'm a plumber's wife who found herself desperately in need of a plumber! I phoned my husband at his shop, and he said he was tied up all day, one of his men was out sick, and the other one was on vacation.

Know what I did? I called another plumber. And in case you don't know it, a plumber gets paid more for a housecall than a doctor.

PLUMB OUT OF LUCK

DEAR ABBY: Tell the doctor's wife she has company. My husband is a professional photographer. He photographed our first child when she was one hour old. And he took thousands of pictures of her until she was about four.

When our second baby came along my husband didn't go quite so crazy with his camera over number 2, but we do have some pictures of him. Number 3 was lucky to get her picture taken on her fifth birthday.

Now I have to start nagging him in July to get a family picture for our Christmas cards.

PHOTOGRAPHER'S WIFE

— ♥ —

The Greeks, who had a word for everything, provided us with a lovely one to describe the sleekly rounded, well-proportioned bottom. In five flowing syllables, the word "callipygian" says it all and says it ever so much more suavely than does the lame literal rendering, "having beautiful buttocks."

Preoccupation with the size and shape of the backside, then, is clearly nothing new. Venus de Milo, an old song says, "was noted for her charms." Less well known but also noted is the callipygian Venus, whose charming derriere once drove the ancient Romans mad.

All of this was updated, in pretty stark terms, when a reader signed "Flat in Back" wrote to me in desperation asking, "Do you know where I can buy a foam-rubber fanny?"

I replied that I had never heard of poopdeck falsies, but if I did I would fill her in with a view toward filling her out.

Some funny feedback on "Flat in Back's" query:

DEAR ABBY: What won't they think of next? Foam-rubber fannies yet! I thought it was a gag, but now I read in your column that they actually make such things.

Of course when you come right down to it, a fake fanny is no more misleading than "falsies," which I understand are very popular.

I appreciate a nice round figure as much as the next guy, but having to guess whether a girl's shape in front is all hers is bad enough without having to wonder if her rump is real. So how can a guy tell for sure?

PEDRO

DEAR PEDRO: In a pinch he can.

DEAR ABBY: Please tell "Flat in Back," who wants a "false fanny," she doesn't know when she's well off. I'd like to know how to get rid of the 180-pound one I have. And it's not foam rubber either. Thank you.

RUTH IN DULUTH

DEAR ABBY: The lady who wants to know where she can

find a foam-rubber fanny is lucky. She has all her problems behind her.

Those forward-looking engineers in the foundation industry seem to have dedicated themselves to the proposition that "it's what's up front that counts."

Not so. A few years back, several manufacturers came out with a false derriere. (One such item, appropriately named "Fancy That," is still on the market.)

I won't say that the demand for such an item hit bottom, but almost no one makes them anymore. So it would seem that these "bras" for the fanny were a bust.

WILLIAM B. GLEESON

DEAR ABBY: I'm glad you told "Flat in Back" about foam-rubber fannies. I know they exist because I saw one advertised in a catalog—and would you believe, it's called "The Living End"!

BARRIE

In response to "Barrie's" letter came this one:

DEAR ABBY: Tell "Barrie" that a foam-rubber fanny can hardly be called "The Living End." It's more like the *dead* end.

LEE

DEAR ABBY: What with foam-rubber fannies, pretty soon the government will force women to wear a "truth in packaging" label.

Can't you just see a guy asking a girl for her government-stamped verification card on which he would read:

Hair: Natural color—gray. Dyed blond or wears a wig.

Teeth: Phony in front. Wears partial plate.

Bust: Actual measurement 20½. Padded to measure 36.
Hips: Actual measurement 22. Padded to measure 38.
Boy, what a revelation! If they ever pass a law like that a lot of women will be in trouble.

LIKES 'EM REAL

Then a feminist reader wrote in demanding equal space:

DEAR ABBY: For "Likes 'Em Real," who got in such a flap over foam-rubber fannies, etc., and suggested "truth in packaging" or verification cards for the ladies, may I suggest one for the gentlemen, too? One might read:

Hair: Natural color—gray. Uses hair color. Also wears hairpiece to cover baldness.

Eyes: Near-sighted. Wears contact lenses.

Teeth: Dentures. (Lost his own when hit in mouth after the "pinch test" for foam-rubber fannies.)

Shoulders: Natural width—32″. With padded shoulders in jacket—44″.

Chest: Actual measurement—32″. With abdominal belt—44″.

Waist: Actual measurement—44″. With abdominal belt—32″.

Height: 5′8″. With elevated shoes—6′1″.

Many men could be in trouble under the same law, if it were passed. Right?

FEMINIST

— ❤ —

Occasionally, an item in the column will touch off a wave of confessions from coast to coast.

A woman in the San Francisco Bay area wrote me one such catalyst letter:

DEAR ABBY: I came across a strongbox full of letters in the trunk of our car. The letters were from a married woman who is in love with my husband. They are so full of mush and love talk it would nauseate you. Should I send the letters to *her* husband and let him handle it in his own way?

BOILING OVER

I wrote her a note suggesting that she fight her own fight with her own husband and leave the other woman's husband out of it. And so to other things, dismissing "Boiling Over" from my mind.

Within the next few days no fewer than thirty letters arrived, bearing postmarks as far apart as Boston and Honolulu, all from women "owning up" to having written the mushy letters. And not one of them lived anywhere near the "scene of the crime"!

The confessions all went like this—

DEAR ABBY: If that woman who found the love letters to her husband will contact me, I can straighten out a few things for her. I also have a lot of letters from *her* husband.

NO HOME WRECKER (BOSTON)

DEAR ABBY: Please inform that lady who found my letters to her husband that if she turns them over to my husband it won't do her any good, because I have already confessed everything and he has forgiven me.

FORGIVEN (CHICAGO)

DEAR ABBY: Please ask that woman who found the box of love letters in her husband's car how much she will take for them. I am sure this concerns me.

WILLING TO BUY (HOUSTON)

DEAR ABBY: You ran a letter from a lady who found a box of letters in the trunk of her husband's car. I pray every night she will take your advice because I am that woman. If this woman who found the letters will destroy the letters without telling my husband, I promise never to see her husband again.

ASKING FOR ANOTHER CHANCE (LOS ANGELES)

In an effort to help a hairdresser with a small problem I ran this brief message:

CONFIDENTIAL TO THE WOMAN WHO SLIPPED HER HAIRDRES- SER'S FAVORITE BRUSH INTO HER PURSE: You were seen. Take the brush back to the shop and quietly leave it in the booth. No questions will be asked.

It resulted in a curious collection of confessions. In all, perhaps forty-five or fifty startled hairdressers suddenly "found" lost hairbrushes. A sampling of the letters I received revealed a number of tender consciences.

DEAR ABBY: A few weeks ago you had an item in your column telling the party who had picked up the beauty operator's favorite hairbrush to return it quietly and there would be no questions asked, as someone had witnessed her little stunt. Well, Abby, I am not the beauty operator who wrote to you with that problem, but someone did steal my favorite hairbrush about a year ago, and one day last week it suddenly was back in my drawer. So thanks a lot.

CLOYD KOOP, BEVERLY HILLS

DEAR ABBY: Talk about coincidence! A hairbrush bearing my initials in nail polish was mailed to me (no return address) in care of the beauty parlor where I was employed over four years ago! I am no longer at that shop, but the package was forwarded to me. I couldn't figure it out as it was just an ordinary hairbrush and I never even missed it. The mystery was solved when some of my operators told me about an article which ran in your column about a month ago. Although I am not the person who wrote to you about the missing hairbrush, I thought you might get a laugh out of knowing that someone apparently had a very guilty conscience.

MADELINE IN ATLANTIC CITY

DEAR ABBY: Would you please put my mind at ease and put a "Confidential" message in your column to "Just Wondering"? Answer either yes or no. Was the lady who was seen slipping a hairbrush into her purse from St. Paul, Minnesota? Thank you.

JUST WONDERING

DEAR WONDERING: No—but return it anyway.

The Funny Ones

Nathanael West, in his poignant novel *Miss Lonelyhearts*, left us an unforgettable portrait of a sensitive newspaperman utterly crushed by the weight of the troubles he saw in the grim business of conducting what used to be called an "advice to the lovelorn" column. Tragedy on tragedy, culminating in the tragedy of poor Miss Lonelyhearts himself.

Miss Lonelyhearts is a literary masterpiece, or so the critics seem to agree. But as a representation of how a "lovelorn" column goes, the picture is not without flaws. The late Mr. West, who saw the world dark and dealt in despair as a matter of practice, forgot the saving grace of humor. It was not his cup of tea, nor that of his forlorn protagonist, who, we are led to believe, went from payday to slender payday without a relieving laugh in between.

Mr. West notwithstanding, people *are* funny. It does us no harm to laugh at them and, as we share humanity, laugh at ourselves. A couple of chuckles a day, which is the least you can expect from a lovelorn column, would have saved Miss Lonelyhearts and ruined Mr. West's novel. He did not let this happen. Agony he was after, and agony he got.

It is also worth noting that a tougher minded Miss Lonelyhearts, one who could laugh and bring healing laughter to his sorry clients, might have accomplished something useful with his life. But he didn't, and alas, the poor guy gloomed along and came to grief.

It made a great novel. But I couldn't have written it. I take the view that not only is it good for us to laugh at the more absurd letter writers, it's good for them, too. Sometimes it's shock treatment. It helps get a problem into perspective once it's cut down to a size that can be managed.

Those who write "the funny ones" don't mean to be funny, but their letters somehow come out that way. As can be expected, the funny ones come from people who range all the way from slightly peculiar to those who are clearly not playing with a full deck.

But they all have one thing in common. They're in dead earnest:

DEAR ABBY: Alfred doesn't drink much, but he sure must have been drunk to do what he did last night. He came home with a pair of lady's lips tattooed on his behind!

He claims he paid the artist to give him a rose.

Is there any way of getting a tattoo removed? I hope so, because Alfred goes to religious retreat camp every summer for two weeks, and he will have to leave soon for camp, and he is ashamed of that tattoo back there.

LILLIAN

— ♥ —

DEAR ABBY: My lady friend is a kissing fool. Hugging and kissing is her idea of the utmost in ecstasy, and she can't seem to get enough of it.

Last night we sat on her sofa kissing from midnight until 2 A.M., and I hardly managed to get my own lips together once in those two hours. If my nose had been stopped up, I would have suffocated. All this time she was glued to my face, wearing me out.

I tried to explain that a normal man enjoys about five minutes of kissing, but I never got to finish the sentence.

It's not as if we are a pair of starry-eyed teen-agers, either. We are up in years.

Is there such a thing as a lip fetish? If so, this lady has a serious case. She doesn't need a man. Give her a pair of rubber lips nailed to a post and she would be in business.

Do you think she needs psychiatric help to cool her down? Or should I seek some myself for continuing to put up with her?

DONE IN

DEAR ABBY: A couple of women moved in across the hall from me. One is a middle-aged gym teacher and the other is a social worker in her mid-twenties. These two women go everywhere together and I've never seen a man go into their apartment or come out. Do you think they could be Lebanese?

CURIOUS

DEAR ABBY: My husband, Elmer, is a pigeon fancier. He belongs to pigeon clubs, goes to meetings, gets all the literature, and, of course, we keep pigeons.

If we go anyplace, it's over to some other pigeon fancier's house. I sit in the car while Elmer looks at birds and talks pigeon talk.

The last time we were somewhere that didn't have something to do with pigeons was at the Elks Club last New Year's Eve. Elmer doesn't care to socialize with anyone unless they have pigeons.

Maybe I'm dumb, Abby, but even though it seems like all I am is a housekeeper, cook, someone to sleep with, I still love him. What should I do.?

SICK OF PIGEONS

DEAR ABBY: My husband was born tired, but somehow he gets the strength to be a twenty-four-hour-a-day lover.

Abby, I've always been a virtuous woman, never shirking my wifely duties, but I pick cotton all day and when nighttime comes I could just drop in my tracks. There is no peace living with a man who has just set and rested up all day, waiting for bedtime. I turn to God on Sundays but need help the other six days, too.

Now I am all wore out, but my man is still going strong. Worse yet, he will not take a bath but once a month. His teeth are rotten, and his breath could kill you dead, but he presents himself for romance every night like he was a teenager.

Don't tell me to take him to a doctor. You don't take a bull no place. In closing, I remain,

Very truly yours,
WORN OUT IN ALABAMA

DEAR WORN OUT: Next Sunday, when you turn to God, pray for strength to see you through the rest of the week.

DEAR ABBY: I wanted to call up my postmaster and tell him a thing or two because I knew he ate my pension check, but I couldn't find his telephone number in the book. I called information, and that's when I found out he had an unlisted number! That really made me mad, so since I knew where he lived, I drove to his house and told his wife off.

Abby, as a taxpayer, I would like to know why a public servant like a postmaster would have an unlisted telephone number?

TAXPAYER

I told "Taxpayer" it was probably to protect him from people who "know" he ate their pension checks.

— ♥ —

DEAR ABBY: My husband and I have been having a little domestic trouble so I finally got him to go to a marriage counselor with me. We were advised to take an interest in each other's hobbies. Well, I'm trying, but it makes me sick to my stomach to go down to the city dump and shoot rats. My husband gets in training for deer hunting this way. Must I join him in this sport?

NO SHOOTER

— ♥ —

Humor is not very far from pathos, but I broke up when I read this pathetic letter:

DEAR ABBY: For my forty-fifth wedding anniversary my husband bought me a plot in the cemetery. Now maybe I shouldn't have said all the things I did to him, but how would you have felt if you were expecting a sewing ma-

chine?
DISAPPOINTED IN BISMARCK

As a sequel to that letter, I heard from a very sympathetic gentleman who wrote:

DEAR ABBY: I just read about that poor woman whose husband bought her a plot in the cemetery when she expected a sewing machine, and I think that's about the cruelest thing a man could have done.
A SINGER SEWING MACHINE SALESMAN

But not to be outdone, I heard from the Necci Sewing Machine people:

DEAR ABBY: With regard to that woman whose husband bought her a plot in the cemetery when she wanted a sewing machine. Tell her we'll make a deal with her. We'll give her a sewing machine free if she'll give us the plot. I think some of our salesmen are dead!

— ♥ —

More pathos:

DEAR ABBY: My husband has a terminal illness. The doctor said they don't know how long he'll last. Would it be proper for me to wear a large black picture hat with a wide brim and a black sheer veil over it for his funeral? My friend says veils are worn only with small hats, but I am a large woman and don't look good in small hats. Also, could I wear a black tailored gabardine suit with a green and blue flowered blouse? Or must I wear all black? If I wear all black, would it be all right to wear one large piece of costume jewelry? And if I wore black hose and black gloves would people think I was overdoing it?

PREPARING AHEAD

I told "Preparing" not to go overboard on getting an outfit together—he might live!

Although I've been warned repeatedly against preaching law in my column, I couldn't resist offering some practical legal advice:

DEAR ABBY: I am a male, age thirty-two. My parents had me circumcised when I was an infant. We are Christians, so there was no religious reason for having maimed me in this manner.

I feel that subjecting a helpless child to such barbaric surgery is an assault on his person and a violation of his rights, and I am seriously considering suing my parents for $100,000 for having permanently disfigured me.

Has a suit of this kind ever been filed?

SERIOUS IN N.Y.

I told "Serious" to go ahead and sue, and if he won he could call it "severance pay."

On the heels of the above came this one:

DEAR ABBY: First, some clown wants to sue his parents for $100,000 for circumcising him when he was an infant. Then someone else writes in and suggests that his mother sue

the idiot for "womb rent." If she does she might as well
try to get carrying charges too.

DALE IN HOOD RIVER, OREGON

DEAR DALE: It seems only fair, since the mother was also
stuck with the delivery charges.

Alas, I had to call on my legal consultants when a Long
Island man wrote to ask if he could sue a hospital for an
inexcusable mistake. He went in for a hemorrhoidectomy
and they straightened his nose.

DEAR ABBY: Is there a law against what you can put in a
person's casket when you bury him?

I have a good friend who made me promise that if he
died before I did, I would get a fifth of the best bourbon
money can buy, take a real big swig, replace the cap, and
put the bottle beside him in the casket.

I told him I would gladly do this, but I need to know if
there is a law against it in Michigan.

NORMAN IN DETROIT

DEAR NORMAN: Any undertaker can tell you. And so can a
Michigan lawyer. (I wonder what your friend has in mind?
Spirits for the spirits, maybe?)

There's no sense in crying over spilled milk:

DEAR ABBY: A young man called me up, saying he got my

name from the La Leche League—an organization to which I belong that provides mother's milk for babies. This man said that his wife had died in childbirth and his baby needed mother's milk.

Being a nursing mother for the La Leche League, I agreed to help him out. I pressed the milk out of my breasts and put in into jars. Then the man stopped by to pick it up. After a few weeks, he broke down and confessed that there was no baby—that *he* had been drinking the milk himself because he has an ulcer and was told that mother's milk would help relieve the pain. Then he had the nerve to ask me if I would let him nurse *direct!* He said he isn't interested in sex—only milk. Is this possible?

ANDREA

I told "Andrea" it was possible, but to tell the young man that goat's milk is also good for ulcers and to find himself another goat!

— ♥ —

DEAR ABBY: First let me explain that I am forty-six and my husband, Frank, is fifty-two. I have a dear friend about my age who lost her husband four years ago, and she's had a bad case of nerves ever since. She told me that her doctor told her that all she needed was a man.

Now I hope you won't think I'm a terrible person, Abby, but when my friend kind of hinted around that she would like to borrow my Frank once in a while to quiet her nerves, I really didn't see anything so wrong with it.

To tell you the truth, I never was very affectionate, and I always felt like Frank got cheated in that department somewhat.

No one would have to know. Do you think I'm crazy?

FRANK'S WIFE

I told "Frank's Wife" that I didn't know whether she was "crazy" or not but I did think she was awfully generous.

And then there are the slightly eccentric and the decidedly "wacko":

DEAR ABBY: My husband is a fine man and an excellent provider, but he has some odd ideas. For example, when we go out for an evening, he orders a vodka martini with eight olives. Then one by one he puts the olives in his nose and sniffs out the juice. (He claims it clears his sinuses.)

I don't mind when he does this at home, but when he does it in public, I want to crawl into a hole. Do you think he should see a psychiatrist?

RADIOLOGIST'S WIFE

I told "Wife" yes, but he should find one who drinks martinis with a twist of lemon so they wouldn't fight over the olives.

DEAR ABBY: My husband's sister is very musical. She is also a little nuts. She plays the guitar and makes up songs. She made up a ballad which she calls, "The Men in My Life." It has about thirty verses and she goes on and on naming one guy after another. Maybe it's true and maybe it's not, but she sure included a lot of guys, both single and married. I told her she'd better quit singing that song around town or she's apt to get herself in a lot of trouble. (She could get sued, couldn't she?) And by the way, how much would it cost to send her to the city to get her head read?

WONDERING IN NASHVILLE

DEAR ABBY: When our daughter was a baby, I found her pacifier in our bed. I thought it had dropped out of her mouth while she was in our bed, but later I found the pacifier in the drawer of our nightstand table, and I couldn't for the life of me figure out how it got there.

Then one morning I woke up early and saw my husband sound asleep with the pacifier in his mouth! We had a good laugh over it, and that evening when I fixed the baby's bottle I jokingly asked him if he wanted a bottle too. He said yes, so I fixed him one.

He loved it, so I kept fixing him a bottle right along with the baby's. I took the baby off the bottle when she was fourteen months old, but my husband still has one every night, and he is thirty-seven. Please don't use our names as my husband is well known here. He works on the space program. Thank you.

HAPPY WIFE

DEAR ABBY: What's my problem? My husband doesn't want me to talk to him. Gerhard asks me not to talk to him during mealtime because he's "busy" eating. He doesn't want me to talk to him while he's driving because he's "busy" driving. And God forbid I should try to talk to him while he's busy reading or watching TV!

Abby, this is very hard on me, because I come from a talkative Jewish family and I love to talk. Gerhard is half

Norwegian and half German. He calls me from work every day to find out what was in the mail. Then I get to talk. Please put this in your column. Gerhard never misses "Dear Abby" and it's the only way to tell him what I think.

ESTHER IN FLATBUSH

DEAR ESTHER: If this is the only way of telling Gerhard what you think, your marriage is finished in English, "Kaput" in German, "ferdig" in Norwegian, and "in drerd" in Yiddish.

On love bugs—dead and alive:

DEAR ABBY: Is there anything in insecticides that could excite a man?

Arthur is fifty-five—just the age most men start to slow down, but he's still going strong. He gets especially aroused right after he sprays our property for bugs.

I noticed it last year when we moved into this house. We had ants and roaches, and right after Arthur sprayed he started looking for me and would get so passionate that he didn't care if I did my housework or even cooked. On weekends he sprays sometimes two and three times a day. It's really getting me down.

We live in Florida. What brand of bug bomb will kill the bugs down here without bringing out my husband's manhood so strong?

He uses Raid, TNT, and Rid-a-bug, and they all have the same effect on him. The brands that don't affect him don't have any effect on the bugs either. Please help me.

TIRED

My chemical experts knew of nothing in any brand of

insecticide that would rejuvenate the waning desire of a man. I told "Tired" if there were, we'd have a lot more dead bugs, livelier husbands, and tired wives.

— ♥ —

Some people don't have a problem, but they do have an urge to write just to get something off their chests: And I'm elected.

DEAR ABBY: While driving through a small city in upstate New York I became ill and a doctor hospitalized me for fifteen days. I was in this semiprivate room and had a "roommate."

My first "roomie" was a ten-year-old kid who watched TV round the clock. I was trapped in an oxygen tent and almost lost my mind.

My next "roomie" was brought into my room at 3 A.M. He'd had a snootful and missed a curve at seventy miles per hour. His wife tore in, hysterical, and proceeded to chew him out. She called him some interesting names, immediately repented, then stood outside the door and cried for two hours while her mother gave her the old "I-told-you-so" routine.

That afternoon about five hundred relatives came to visit him. At least a dozen of them pulled out cigarettes and were just about to light up when they were calmly told that the "guy in the other bed" was in an oxygen tent! I kept expecting to be blown to bits any minute. After they left, his wife sat on his bed and cried for another two hours.

By this time I was begging the nurses to put me in a morgue so I could get some rest.

Somehow I got well enough to go home.

Thanks for letting me get this off my chest, Abby. I had

to tell somebody or burst.

STANLEY FROM ALBANY

DEAR ABBY: I am a woman over forty, self-supporting, and never married, and I live alone. I'm active in my church and have some nice friends, mostly church people. I never really wanted boyfriends and am happy with my life, except for some strong moods I get into once in a while.

Sometimes I wish someone would turn me over their knee and give me a good, hard spanking. I have tried spanking myself with a wooden spoon but it wasn't very effective. A leather strap would be better.

Don't get me wrong. I'm no nut. I just occasionally feel the need of a good, sound spanking on my bare bottom with a leather strap, but if I were to ask someone to do this they would think I am off my rocker.

WANTS TO BE SPANKED

DEAR ABBY: I went to my minister because I have been having marital problems with my husband. It had to do with lovemaking. (He wasn't doing any.) I'm twenty-eight and he's twenty-nine.

The minister said he really didn't know all that much about the subject, but he suggested that I take some belly-dancing lessons to entertain my husband, and maybe that would perk him up a little.

Do you know of any place in Asheville, N.C., that teaches belly dancing?

WILLING TO LEARN

DEAR ABBY: What am I to do? While I was clerking part-time in a department store, a middle-aged man walked over to my counter and didn't say a word, he just stood directly in front of me and winked at me! I was working in intimate apparel and happened to have a lady's corset in my hand at the time, so I slapped him across the face with it. A metal garter caught him in the eye and cut his eyeball slightly. He didn't go blind or anything like it, but he is suing the store.

I lost my job because it turned out that this man is a very respectable citizen with a nervous tic and he meant no harm. I am a widow in my sixties and need to work.

LUCKLESS

DEAR LUCKLESS: If the man had had no nervous tic and actually winked at you, it still wouldn't have justified your slapping him with a corset. You should have called the manager.

It's lucky you weren't in "housewares." You might have parted his hair with a skillet.

— ♥ —

DEAR ABBY: I just read the letter from the twenty-eight-year-old mother of four who tacked a poster on her door with "rules" to keep visitors away.

Well, I'm a thirty-eight-year-old mother of six, and I'm amazed that anyone would want that much privacy. We're newcomers who live in the country, and I'm stuck out here with six kids, two dogs, and three cats. I'm so hungry for company, I'm ready to go out on the road and flag down some strangers.

Please print my "poster" in the paper for all to read:

—You may smoke inside, outside, on the roof, or any-where you wish, just don't burn the house down.

—If you're hungry, help yourself to anything you can find. And if you can't find anything, ask one of the kids. They'll fix you a peanut butter and brown sugar sandwich.

—If you're here around mealtime, grab a chair and join us.

—If you want to stay overnight, bring a sleeping bag and we'll move some clutter from the corner to make room for you.

—Bring your kids. We have so many, a few more won't make any difference.

—We can't lend you any money, but go ahead and ask anyway. It will make us feel good to know we appear that prosperous.

—Tell us your troubles and we'll tell you ours. One of our kids can play the violin for background music, and we can all cry together.

—If you can stand us, we can stand you, so drop in anytime and stay as long as you like. We're people who like people.

MIDGE IN WATSONVILLE, CAL.

DEAR MIDGE: You sound like the kind of person I'd like to know. I'll bet you won't be hungry for company long.

DEAR ABBY: Anybody who thinks women have equal rights in this country is crazy.

If a man's trousers are too tight, he's just put on a little weight. (If a woman's skirt is too tight, she's trying to be sexy.)

If a man stands on a street corner, he's getting some fresh air. (If a woman stands on a corner, she's looking to be picked up.)

If a man has one drink too many, he's "feeling good." (If a woman has one drink too many, she's a lush.)

If a man has a night out with the boys, he's put in a hard day at work and needs to "relax." (If a woman has a night out with the girls, she's up to no good and should stay home with her family.)

If a man cheats on his wife, people say he's probably married to a cold fish and he's only human. (If a woman cheats, she's a tramp.)

If a kid turns out good, he's a chip off the old block. (If he turns out bad, his mother did the rotten job of raising him.)

Wouldn't you say it's still a man's world, Abby?

WANTS EQUALITY

DEAR WANTS: Only if he's single. If he's married, almost everything is in his wife's name.

DEAR ABBY: Our nineteen-year-old daughter, Caroline, has started going with a guy named Angelo. He never takes her anyplace. He just comes over every night to watch television and wear out our sofa.

When Angelo comes over, the wife and I have to go sit in the kitchen so he and Caroline can have their privacy in the living room. I suppose we could go into our bedroom, but who wants to go to bed at seven o'clock?

So, every night lately the wife and I sit in the kitchen like a couple of cockroaches trying to watch television on a dinky little portable.

The wife is so happy that Caroline finally has a boyfriend she doesn't say a word. I am getting tired of this setup. What should I do?

KITCHEN SITTER

DEAR SITTER: Send me a picture of Caroline and I'll tell you what to do.

DEAR ABBY: I am a Taurus very much in love with a Scorpio.

First, let me explain that before I knew anything about the zodiac, I foolishly married a Sagittarius, so our marriage was doomed from the start.

My Scorpio married an Aries (an impossible union). They would have made excellent business partners, but their temperaments were all wrong for marriage.

Anyway, my Scorpio has left his Aries, but I can't get rid of my Sagittarius. I'd divorce him but I have no grounds, and he won't divorce me, although he has all the grounds he needs.

My horoscope says I should make no important decisions of the heart until after the first of next year but I just can't see spending another Christmas with this miserable man.

                                                                Taurus

— ♥ —

What's in a name? Plenty, I learned. At least that's the message I get from some of my readers. Three outstanding letters come to mind:

DEAR ABBY: I am a direct descendant of General Joseph Hooker, who served valiantly in the Civil War.

I don't know how my family name became a synonym for prostitute, whore, or harlot, but I find it very offensive.

There are numerous other Hookers who are respectable, law-abiding citizens, and I am sure I speak for them when I say we Hookers are slandered by this commonly accepted, immoral connotation.

My son is seriously considering changing his name because his fiancee doesn't want to be a "Hooker," and she says if she has daughters she doesn't want them to be "Hookers," either.

Am I overly sensitive? Or have I a point?

AN OFFENDED HOOKER

DEAR ABBY: My family name is "Gay." My ancestors have been traced back to France in the early sixteen hundreds.

I am writing this in the hopes that the Gay Liberation Society will see it and realize how unfair they are to use our name for their organization.

Since the homosexuals have organized and officially adopted our name for their group, we have been harassed with crank telephone calls at all hours and subjected to insults and ridicule.

Our name was "Gay" long before they took that name, so I think in all fairness to us Gays they should change the name of their society to one more befitting to their crusade.

A PROUD GAY

DEAR PROUD: I understand your plight but I doubt if the Gay Liberation Society will consider changing its name. Although you were Gay first, I believe there are more of them than there are of you.

DEAR ABBY: We named our son "John" after his father. His grandfather, great-grandfather, and great-great-grandfather were also Johns. Abby, our son is named after a person—not a toilet!

Will you please tell me when, where and how the toilet came to be known as a john? Thank you.

WIFE AND MOTHER OF A JOHN
NOT A TOILET

In researching the subject, I learned more about toilets than I cared to know. I found several conflicting theories on how the toilet came to be known as "the john," the most reasonable explanation being that the first toilet was called "john" after its English inventor back in the early eighteen hundreds.

I bought it, after checking it out with a plumber in Flushing.

— ♥ —

Seconds, anyone?

DEAR ABBY: My husband's brother is the kind who will walk into your house, head right for the refrigerator, and help himself. It has always burned me up, but I've never said anything. Sunday Ned did that stunt again. He took out a bowl of liver and mashed potatoes I had scraped off everybody's plates and mixed for cat food. I was saving it for my neighbor's cat, which I am feeding while she is on vacation. Well, Ned made himself a big sandwich of this stuff, got himself a beer, and seemed to enjoy it. I never said a word until he got all through, and then I told him what he ate. I am not going to tell you what happened after that, Abby, but I laughed so hard I cried. Ned isn't talking to me and neither is my husband. Did I do anything so terrible? The stuff was fresh and wouldn't have killed anybody.

ELSIE

I told "Elsie" I thought it was hilarious. But she could have waited a few days to tell him.

DEAR ABBY: The letter from apartment dwellers who can't sleep because of the noisy mattress acrobatics of the couple upstairs calls to mind my husband's famous faux pas:

We had that problem with the Smiths, whose bedroom was directly over ours.

The first time my husband ran into Mr. Smith, he told him with a knowing wink that their noisy nocturnal lovemaking had been interfering with our sleep.

My husband received an icy stare.

We later learned that Mr. Smith worked nights.

FOOT IN MOUTH IN CHICAGO

From sunny Italy a small request:

DEAR ABBY: I am an Italian man, age thirty-four. I am medium build and am told that I am good-looking. I drive a sightseeing bus by day, so I speak a little English. I am single and would like to correspond with an American woman between the ages of thirty and sixty.

She doesn't have to be beautiful, but I want one who has a steady income and owns a late model American automobile.

If you know of a woman who would like to correspond with me, please ask her to send a picture of the automobile.

VITO IN NAPOLI

Some nuggets from my "How was that again, please?" file:

... My neighbor is getting married in the spring. She's a Catholic and he's an alcoholic.

... I suspected that my husband had been fooling around, and when I confronted him with the evidence he denied everything and said it would never happen again.

... My husband burns the hair out of his nose with a lighted match, and he thinks I'm crazy because I voted for Goldwater!

... Will you please *rush* me the name of a reliable illegitimate doctor?

... While my husband was in the service, he lived with a native woman off the post for two years. When he left home he told me he couldn't take his wife along. Will you please tell me how this bum got the good-conduct medal?

... Our son writes that he is taking Judo. Why would a boy who was raised in a good Christian home turn against his own?

... I joined the Navy to see the world. I've seen it. Now how do I get out?

... My forty-year-old son has been paying a psychiatrist $50 an hour every week for two-and-a-half years. He must be crazy.

... What suggestion do you have for preventing foot rot in feeder cattle? I have it every year.

... I have met a woman who is perfect for me in every way. With her I can find the happiness I've always dreamed of. However, I still feel an obligation to the woman I'm married to.

... Now a little about my family. I have three brothers. One is living and two are married.

... I was married to Bill for three months and I didn't know he drank until one night he came home sober.

... I hear there's a sex revolution going on. Will you please tell me where it is and how I get there?

... Do you think it would be all right if I gave my doctor a little gift? I tried for years to get pregnant and couldn't, and he finally did it.

... My husband has beaten me up so many times I'm ashamed to call the police again. I couldn't go anywhere if I wanted to, as I have no money, no job, and besides I need a permanent.

... My husband has only one kidney, 25 percent of his stomach, no gall bladder, dizzy spells, and various other things. Fortunately he inherited a very strong constitution. Otherwise he'd probably be dead by now.

... I have seen four different parish priests so far this year and couldn't get anywhere with them. So could you please send me Pope Paul's home address?

— ♥ —

The following "funny ones" were answered in a straight-faced humorless manner because in every case the writer was absolutely sincere:

DEAR ABBY: I took your advice and decided to start the day out by being real nice to my husband, so first thing in the morning, I said "Good morning, darling. I love you and, my, but I am glad you are mine." He just looked at me and said, "What's the matter with you? Are you still drunk?"

... I know for sure that salt peter slows down a man's sexual urge because my husband had some during World War II and it's just now beginning to take effect.

DEAR ABBY: My wife is a little squirrely. It runs in her family. Fifty years after the Civil War was over her great-grandfather shot a postman thinking he was a Confederate soldier.

Some excerpts from young writers who didn't realize how funny they were.

Tonight at the supper table my father said, "Pass the salt." I passed it to him. Then I said, "Dad, isn't it proper to say 'please' when you want something passed?" Abby, how do you get the swelling to go down on your lip?

I'm a big fan of yours, Abby. I heard you speak at our high school assembly last year and you even made sex sound clean.

I think it's just plain lewd to let people gaze at your naked body except in the cases of sickness and marriage.

DEAR ABBY: Socrates was a very smart man. They poisoned him. Please be careful.

Love,
ALLEN

I always wanted be become a nun until my girlfriend introduced me to her cousin.

My mother is mean and short-tempered. I think she is going through her mental pause.

I met this nice guy who was in the service. He's the chief petting officer.

DEAR ABBY: You are solving my problem without even noing it becuz I choze you to rite to.

I think you rite a real good columb. I don't always agree with your ansers but then nobody is perfeck. I shure give you a lot of credit. It takes a lot of guts to tell people what to do becuz you no what happens to people who stik there nose in other people's biznus.

Yours truly,
F IN ENGLISH

One seven-year-old boy wrote to complain bitterly about Phyllis, his eleven-year-old tyrannical sister. On the back of his letter I noticed, printed in a childish scrawl:

Things to do
1) Get pencil box
2) Cub Scout kerchief
3) Find mitten
4) Kill Phyllis

The Sad Ones

Because my column is a "trouble dump," I could fill it daily with tales of tragedy told by people who agonize in detail over their misfortunes. But today when so much human misery is brought into our homes routinely as part of the six o'clock news, I prefer to use more cheerful letters than sad ones.

Of course, I print some of the "sad ones," because to eliminate them would be unrealistic and dishonest. Besides, misery really does love company and those who are suffering hurt a little less when they know that others are suffering too.

If the soap opera writers ever run out of material, as a public service to all those hooked housewives I might be willing to let the scriptwriters read my mail. Some of the convoluted situations described in my mail contain enough material to provide the networks with television serials indefinitely.

So, if you don't feel like weeping, perhaps you'd better

skip "The Sad Ones." This is a three-hanky chapter. Trust me.

DEAR ABBY: I have never written before but I think the following might interest you and some of your readers:

Yesterday was an old man's birthday. He was ninety-one, and "home" was a small rented room with cooking privileges. He awakened earlier than usual, bathed, shaved, and put on his best clothes. Surely they would come today, he thought.

He wouldn't take his daily walk to the gas station to visit with the old-timers of the neighborhood because he wanted to be right here when they came.

He sat on the front porch with a clear view of the road so he could see them coming. Surely they would come today.

He'd skip his noon nap that day, because he wanted to be up when they came.

He has six children. Two of his daughters and their married children live within a few miles. They hadn't been to see him for a long time, and today was his birthday. Surely they would come.

At suppertime, his landlady brought him some ice cream and a small cake, but he didn't eat it. He was saving it to have with "them" when they came.

Nighttime came, and the old gentleman went to his room to retire. But first he knocked on his landlady's door and said, "Promise to wake me when they come."

It was his birthday and he was ninety-one.

HIS LANDLADY

DEAR ABBY: My forty-two-year-old husband has been suffering from a muscle-deteriorating disease for the past eleven years. He hasn't been able to walk for four years, so he's confined to a wheelchair.

I work outside my house and in addition to being a nurse to my husband, I am raising three children.

I am forty, attractive, and I miss dancing, swimming, and bowling, which I once loved. Would it be wrong for me to accept the occasional companionship of a man who can do all those things I love to do? I don't want to get emotionally involved with another man because I love my husband, but, Abby, I get so weary just sitting with him.

What do other wives of handicapped husbands do? I am a normal, healthy, energetic woman. Please don't give me a sermon about having taken this man "in sickness and in health." I know all that. What I need is some advice.

FRUSTRATED

DEAR FRUSTRATED: If you honestly don't want to become emotionally involved with another man, don't go swimming, dancing, or bowling with one. It may start out innocently enough, but it rarely ends up that way.

After publicizing the Living Will, which is a document stating that when there is no hope for recovery, one reserves the right to die in dignity, I received this reassuring letter:

DEAR ABBY: My husband was in and out of hospitals for twelve years. The last ten months I was at his bedside every day from 7 A.M. until midnight.

I watched him being kept alive with blood transfusions, needles, tubes, and drugs, while he prayed for God to take him. He couldn't swallow. I gave him water with an eyedropper.

This handsome, husky two-hundred-pound man became an eighty-eight-pound vegetable when God finally took him home.

May the day come soon when everyone will be able to die with dignity. Don't let people tell you that you have no right to interfere with God's decision by suggesting that they sign a Living Will. It is they who permit tubes and needles and machines to prolong life artificially when death is inevitable who are interfering with God's will.

I will take the word of my clergyman, doctors, lawyers, and the selected members of my own family when they agree that my life has run its course.

I am not afraid to die, but I never want to put my loved ones through what I went through with my husband. Keep up the good work, Abby. And God bless you.

MRS. W.J.A.

DEAR ABBY: I just can't believe that you took the time to write a personal letter. And when you said, "Please write again. I care," I cried.

Abby, why would anyone want to help me straighten out my rotten mixed-up life? I don't deserve it. Five times people saved me from suicide. Sometimes I wish they'd have let me die—it's so hard to keep saying "thank you."

I'm a registered nurse and should be helping people, but instead people are helping me. I feel so guilty.

I have a fantastic new psychiatrist who acts as though he really cares about me. I don't know why anyone would care if I lived or died. I'm not pretty or smart or productive. I'm a burden and a problem to everyone who knows me. But this doctor makes me feel so great.

Is life worth living to feel great for only one hour a week? Help me.

FINISHED AT TWENTY-FOUR

DEAR TWENTY-FOUR: You're far from finished, you're just beginning to realize how precious life is. Every human being who reaches out for help wants it—and deserves it. It's always darkest just before dawn. Hang in there and don't let your doctor (or yourself) down. You can make it if you try. I'm counting on you.

DEAR ABBY: I am a twenty-three-year-old male nurse. I love sports and excelled in track. I was saved by the grace of Jesus Christ two years ago. I read the Bible daily and sing in the gospel choir.

Even though I am a born-again Christian, I am miserable. All my life I have wanted to be a woman. I would love to be on the U.S. Women's Olympic Track Team. I can cook, sew, and type. I have never cared anything about mechanics, engineering, or any of the so-called masculine careers. I hate hunting and fishing. I could never kill a living thing.

Abby, this secret desire to be a woman is about to destroy me. I am not a homosexual, but I'd give anything to have a sex-change operation. Where is this done? Is it against the law? I will go anywhere. I'd rather be dead than continue living like this.

Abby, if the Lord really loves me, why did He give me a man's body when I feel and think like a woman? I have been this way all my life. Please help me!

SAVED BUT DIFFERENT

DEAR SAVED: The Lord created all of us, and why He made you "different" I do not know. Nature sometimes makes biological blunders, as is the case when one's body does not conform with his (or her) natural feelings. You are not alone. Don't feel guilty. One cannot help what he feels.

I believe that knowledge, skill, and talent are divinely

inspired, and that those scientists, physicians, and surgeons whose combined efforts have made sex-change operations possible do so with God's guidance. For information about sex-reassignment surgery and related problems, inquire at the nearest medical school that has a human sexuality program.

DEAR ABBY: I am so worried about my thirty-five-year-old daughter. Tonight she telephoned me long distance in such a weakened state she could hardly talk. Her fourteen-year-old son had lost his temper and beaten her violently with his fists. In the past, he has lied and stolen from her, but no amount of punishment helped. But tonight he almost put my poor daughter in the hospital.

He's an adopted child and I'm afraid he is a mental case. He is big and terribly strong for his age, and I fear one day he will kill somebody. My daughter's husband travels a great deal and she can't handle the boy alone. What should I do?

HEARTSICK

I recommended family counseling. Until then the battered mother was not even aware that such counseling was available through her local mental health clinic.

DEAR ABBY: I knew I wasn't wanted from the time I was old enough to understand English. My father used to beat the daylights out of my mother. She took to drinking and left him many times, but she always went back because of me. My father hated me. I could never do anything right.

I was always in some kind of trouble. I ran away from home several times. At fifteen I ran away for good and had to steal and push drugs to live. I got hooked on heroin and ended up in Lexington, Kentucky, a physical and mental wreck—at age nineteen.

I am not blaming anyone else for the mess I made of my life, but I read your column and I know you reach a lot of people and I wish you would keep telling them that most of the crime and trouble in the world is caused by kids who weren't wanted.

ONE OF THEM

DEAR ABBY: During my childhood I often caught my mother crying. When I was fourteen, she told me, "Never marry a jealous man." I paid little attention. In fact, I gave it no thought until I married one myself.

All the signs were there for me to read, but when you're in love you think your love can conquer all. It can't.

When I married Roy, I was a virgin and he knew it but as far as he was concerned, I could just as well have been a streetwalker. After we were married he repeatedly insulted me, saying it was impossible for a pretty girl to have worked alongside men as I have done and remain a virgin. I should have said goodbye right then and there, but I had been raised to believe that "divorce" was a disgrace. Then Roy started to accuse me of every man I had ever known. I thought a "family" would solve everything, so in five years I had two babies.

Nothing changed. For twenty-two years I lived in hell, but I finally won. Both children have college degrees and have grown up to be worthwhile people. I have kept my mouth shut when the mere effort made my jaws ache.

When the youngest was twenty-one and established, I

walked out on Roy. Since then, I have put him completely out of my life. I heard recently that he had died. The news (if true) leaves me cold. My "husband" died years ago.

Am I disloyal? I don't think so. I am probably writing this to get it off my chest.

I didn't pay any attention to my mother when she told me not to marry a jealous man. And maybe nobody will pay any attention to me. But when that innocent little girl wrote to you saying, "I'm glad my fiance is jealous. It just proves he 'loves' me," I wanted to scream!

That poor little thing. Little does she know that it proves nothing of the sort. Jealousy has nothing to do with love. It's a sickness. And no amount of patience, sacrifice, giving in, or giving up will cure it. I know this is too long for your column, but I just had to have my say.

PEACE AT LAST

DEAR PEACE: It's long, all right, but I didn't have the heart to cut it. Some people do learn from the mistakes of others. You've paid the "tuition"—perhaps a reader will read this and get by on a "scholarship."

DEAR ABBY: My problem is my guilt. I had a very unhappy childhood because my father used to beat my mother (and still does) and he'd beat us kids until we were a mass of welts. I hate him, and can't tell you the number of times I wished him dead. He doesn't drink, and he goes to church, but you'd never know it. He only hits people who can't fight back. He's the cruelest man I know. He went into a rage once after he beat Mom so bad he put her in the hospital.

We are all married now and can't understand why Mom still stays with him. We've all told her she can come and live with any of us.

My husband welcomes my mother in our home, but not my father, because my father once started slapping Mom around in our house and my husband has barred him from our property ever since.

I feel so guilty having a wonderful husband and family and knowing what Mom is putting up with. Thanks for listening.

GUILTY DAUGHTER

DEAR ABBY: Please tell me what to do when a friend has had an abnormal child (a Mongoloid)?

I certainly can't send a card or gift of "congratulations" to someone who has had such a tragedy. Would a message of "sympathy" be more in order? Or should something like this be acknowledged at all?

OKLAHOMAN

DEAR OKLAHOMAN: A child, normal or otherwise, is a child to his mother. Don't differentiate. Send a little gift with your love and best wishes.

Shortly after that item ran I received this one:

DEAR ABBY: "Oklahoman" wrote asking if she should acknowledge the birth of a Mongoloid child. Thank you for saying, "By all means, yes. To a mother, a child is a child."

I know your advice was sound because I had a Mongoloid son. Friends called. They stopped by. They even gave me a surprise baby shower when he was a month old. Here is the message on one card which meant so much to me:

"God gave this child to you to guide,
To love, to walk through life beside.
A little child so full of charms,
To fill a pair of loving arms.
God picked you out because He knew
How safe His child would be with you."
God bless friends like that.

MRS. C. B., BEACON, N.Y.

DEAR ABBY: Concerning the birth of an abnormal child, we were lucky to be told immediately of our baby's condition and did not have the agony of the slow realization that "something was wrong."

Feeling it best to face the problem, we decided to tell our friends and relatives about our "special" child. Although we knew very little about what to expect, he was our baby and we knew we wanted to keep him with us. He is now a lovable, mischievous eleven-year-old Mongoloid, going to a special school, and we have never regretted our decision.

Perhaps "congratulations" are not in order, but to ignore the presence of a new baby in a home, when you would normally express interest, is, I think, cruel. To this day I remember the pleasure I felt when someone came to see our baby, to hold him, and to let me talk about him.

One of the burdens a mother of a retarded child has is not having anyone with whom to compare notes about her child's progress. Every tiny gain has a tremendously important meaning for the mother of a handicapped child.

So, do acknowledge the birth of a special child. Or send a little gift. Or send flowers to the mother. Continue to show an interest (not curiosity), and encourage the parents to get in touch with their local society for retarded children for help with mutual problems. It will be rewarded with much love, affection, and gratitude.

EDITH

DEAR ABBY: I want to say "thank you" for something you did for me.

On May 6, our second son was born. But he was not like our first, healthy, "normal" son. He is Mongoloid. With the help of family, friends, and doctors, I prepared myself for the raising of our "special" child. But the acceptance came much harder for my proud husband. It's easier for a mother to love the child she has carried for nine months, but for the father, that love sometimes comes harder, and after many forced smiles and sleepless nights, my husband now admits that he was miserable. Needlessly miserable, he knows now, but at first he wondered if he could ever "love" his second son as he should.

On May 11, your column concerning Mongoloid babies appeared. It could not have come out at a better time for us. That made the difference in my husband's life. After reading that column, he no longer had that "why-did-this-have-to-happen-to-us" attitude. And just knowing how other people have handled it can help a lot.

Our baby is eight months old now, and a happier child I've never seen. And I know a lot of his happiness comes from knowing that his mother and daddy and brother really love and accept him totally.

Dear, Dear Abby, if you did nothing else this year, you have helped one father find the love he always had for his "special" child. Thank you!

DOUG'S MOTHER

DEAR MOTHER: Your letter made this five-feet-nothing columnist nine feet tall today. After this appears, I know I'll be deluged with requests to reprint the column, so tomorrow, with the kind indulgence of those readers who have already read it, I shall do so.

— ♥ —

DEAR ABBY: I have a problem others may have, so if you answer in your column, others will benefit too.

Seven years ago my husband and I lost our two children in a flash fire. The boy was five and his sister was two. We were away from home at the time. A fifteen-year-old babysitter perished with them. We desperately wanted a new family.

Two years later I gave birth to a brain-damaged son, who died before he was a year old. I became pregnant with twins a few months later and had a miscarriage. I had to have a hysterectomy.

We put in for adoption and were overjoyed to get a newborn baby girl. When our angel was only two months old she died for no apparent reason, leaving us heartbroken and frustrated. They called it a crib death.

Obviously, we have no children, and we probably never will.

My problem: Well-meaning strangers ask upon meeting me: "Have you a family?" Or: "How many children have you?"

This question throws me into a state of depression.

I don't feel like going into my whole tragic history. Abby, please print this so strangers will think twice before asking, "Do you have any children?"

LOST SIX

DEAR ABBY: I am married to a madman. If I fix him breakfast maybe he'll eat it, and maybe he'll throw it at me. If I don't fix him breakfast, he runs down the street, cursing a blue streak. He gets raving mad over nothing and throws the patio furniture a hundred feet over the fence. Then he runs out of the house and hides in alleys.

Don't tell me to call the county authorities. I did and they said, "He sounds sick. Bring him in sometime."

And don't tell me to take him to a psychiatrist. He's too heavy to carry and too big to push. And have you ever tried driving a car with a man who is trying to jump out? You steer with one hand and hold onto his belt with the other and pray he won't jump out into the traffic.

I suppose I could just kill myself to get away from this maniac, but I have no such intentions. For God's sake, Abby, help me! I am tired of hunting for a crazy husband in the alleys with a flashlight at 2 A.M..

MARGARET

Unfortunately, "Margaret" did not give her last name or a clue to where she lived. So I printed her letter urging her to get help from her physician or local police department.

— ♥ —

DEAR ABBY: I am fourteen, and five years ago I was in a car accident. After many operations and much therapy I was able to walk again—but with a noticeable limp.

In that accident we lost my little sister, so my mother, not wanting me to be an "only child," adopted a little girl who had been deaf since birth.

What I'm getting at is this: You've seen comedians on TV or the stage lisping, stuttering, stumbling, falling, and "playing deaf and mute," and they get laughs that bring the house down.

I don't see anything funny about this, and it's not that I'm overly sensitive, because I felt the same way before the accident.

I have seen handicapped people at the rehabilitation center stumbling and falling and doing the same things the comedians do for laughs, and believe me, it's not funny.

My little sister spends hours with a speech therapist

trying to form words, and when she sees someone on TV who makes the same sounds as she, and the people laughing at it, she runs to her room in tears. (She is only five.)

Please let your readers know they shouldn't laugh at handicapped people.

NOT LAUGHING

DEAR ABBY: My husband is dead, and I am all alone in the world. Loneliness is like a cancer, only it's worse. It doesn't kill you, it just gnaws at the mind until concentration and constructive thinking are permanently crippled.

When my husband was living, we visited lonely people and often took them for rides, to the movies, and out for a meal. But now that I am alone, no one visits me or offers to take me anywhere. Married people don't care. They have each other. Sundays are endless.

I am treated worse than a criminal. Perhaps if I were a criminal, some saintly person from a church group would call on me and try to save my "soul."

I used to attend church, but the church pays no attention to my loneliness. I am not rich, neither am I poor. I am not beautiful, nor am I ugly. I'm too old to work and I'm too young to die.

I know there is no solution to my loneliness, but I had to tell somebody.

DYING OF LONELINESS

A sad letter with a happy ending:

DEAR ABBY: I am writing to thank you for saving my life.

In December 1973 I weighed 326 pounds. If my high blood pressure or heart trouble wouldn't have eventually killed me, I'd have done it myself. I lived with loneliness, depression, and despair.

I was a heroin addict and a twenty-three-year-old divorced mother of three on welfare. I hated myself enough to prostitute my body to get money for dope. I suffered humiliation after humiliation. (A three-hundred-pound prostitute gets all the sadists and perverts no other hooker will take.) I had no self-respect, no hope, no God—no nothing.

I wrote to you, never expecting an answer. Your letter was the first word of encouragement I had had in years. You advised me to go to Overeaters Anonymous. I took your advice and went to a meeting in June of '74. I believed none of it. "These people are crazy," I thought. "I'm a fat, ugly junkie, and they're telling me I can get thin and regain my self-respect if I want to!"

"No way," I told them right out loud. No one threw me out. A beautiful, middle-aged man put his arm around my shoulder and said, "Come back and listen. Try us for thirty days. What can you lose?"

I didn't believe him, but I went back, and back, and back.

Today I've lost 121 pounds, and I'm still losing. I'm drug-free, and I'm learning to like myself. I have a responsible job, a belief in a power greater than myself, and the love and respect of my children and people who believed in me when I didn't believe in myself.

There is no scale at O.A. They don't shame you if you backslide. They are a group of loving, caring, supportive people who are there to help you because they have been helped themselves.

After sinking so low, O.A. gave me a chance to be what I've always wanted to be: a lady.

Thank you for sending me there.

"BORN AGAIN" IN CONNECTICUT

DEAR BORN AGAIN: You owe me no thanks. I merely threw you a lifeline. You caught it.

One-Liners

I'm told that one of the reasons my column caught on so quickly was because of the one-liners.

There have been many quotable one-liners in my column over the years, but one stands out as a classic. It was one of my earliest and has been translated into Japanese, German, Italian, French, Danish, and Swedish.

DEAR ABBY: I am a girl who just celebrated her twenty-first birthday. On this occasion my boyfriend took me out to dinner. He doesn't drink much and neither do I, but before dinner we each had three martinis. During dinner (just to celebrate), we split a bottle of champagne. After dinner, we each had four brandies.

Did I do wrong?

BLONDIE

My succinct reply: "Probably."

— ♥ —

Perhaps it's my Jewish heritage, but my humor tends to have a sharp edge, a touch of healthy sarcasm, and I frequently answer a question with another question. As in these:

DEAR ABBY: A woman who was married for forty-six years wrote a long story about how hard her husband was to live with. She asked you whether she should choose divorce or suicide, and she signed herself, "Suffered Enough."

You told her divorce was preferable. Are you married to a divorce lawyer, Abby?

NOSY

DEAR NOSY: No. Are you married to an undertaker?

DEAR ABBY: My husband is in the paint and paper business. A young widow in the next town asked him to paint her kitchen, and he has been doing the job. Abby, he started four months ago and he isn't finished yet. Is this possible?

MARION

DEAR MARION: How big is the lady's kitchen?

DEAR ABBY: I've been going with this girl for a year. How can I get her to say yes?

DON

DEAR DON: What's the question?

DEAR ABBY: What is a good line for a girl to get into if she's interested in finding a man?

ANXIOUS

DEAR ANXIOUS: Airline stewardess—where else can you find a man already strapped down?

DEAR ABBY: I am a girl of fifty-nine and I'm going with a guy of seventy-eight. He says he wants to marry me but his sister won't let him. Don't you think he's old enough to do what he wants to do?

NELLIE

DEAR NELLIE: By all means. But is he young enough?

DEAR ABBY: I've been going steady with this man for six years. We see each other every night. He says he loves me, and I know I love him, but he never mentions marriage. Do you think he's going out with me just for what he can get?

GERTIE

DEAR GERTIE: I don't know. What's he getting?

DEAR ABBY: Why do Jews always answer a question with another question?

DANNY

DEAR DANNY: How else should they answer?

I'll admit that some of my one-liners are more humorous than helpful, but I bravely (and sometimes foolishly) go for the chuckle and risk the wrath of those humorless critics who always take me literally. Some samples:

DEAR ABBY: My problem is my sorority sister. I've fixed her up with several real sharp guys, but they never ask her out again because she's so quiet. They all say it's like pulling teeth to get a word out of her. Any suggestions?

A.E. PHI

DEAR A.E. PHI: Yes. Get her a date with a dental student.

DEAR ABBY: My husband hates to spend money! I cut my own hair and make my own clothes, and I have to account for every nickel I spend. Meanwhile he has a stack of savings bonds put away that would choke a cow. How do I get some money out of him before we are both called to our final judgment? He says he's saving for a rainy day.

FORTY YEARS HITCHED

DEAR HITCHED: Tell him it's raining!

DEAR ABBY: My wife sleeps in the nude. Then she showers, goes into the kitchen and fixes breakfast—still in the nude. We're newlyweds and have no kids, so I suppose there's nothing wrong with it. What do you think?

REX

DEAR REX: It's all right with me, but tell her to put on an apron when she's frying bacon.

DEAR ABBY: My husband lost his wallet. It was mailed back and I found it stuffed with snapshots of other women. I confronted him with this evidence and he said, as a true Southern gentleman, he refused to muddy the names of the ladies in the pictures. What can I do with this Alabama Skunk?

MYRA

DEAR MYRA: Cut off his hominy grits.

DEAR ABBY: I haven't been able to sleep very well lately. You see, I cheated a little on my income tax. (Phony deductions.) Any suggestions?

S.O.S.

DEAR S.O.S.: Yes. Send the IRS $100. And if you still can't sleep, send them the balance.

DEAR ABBY: My boyfriend is going to be twenty years old next month. I'd like to give him something nice for his birthday. What do you think he'd like?

CAROL

DEAR CAROL: Never mind what he'd like. Give him a tie.

DEAR ABBY: What do you say to a niece with brown eyes and coal black hair who is married to a man who also has brown eyes and coal black hair and just gave birth to a baby boy with blue eyes and light blond hair?

CURIOUS UNCLE

DEAR CURIOUS: "Congratulations!"

DEAR ABBY: Another man and I went on a weekend fishing trip. When he came to pick me up, and saw my wife for the first time, his eyes grew wider, and he turned to me and said, "You've gotta be nuts to leave a beautiful thing like her alone for the weekend." Was I?
LIKES TO FISH

DEAR LIKES: I don't know about *that* weekend, but the next time you go fishing be sure to take the same man with you.

DEAR ABBY: Are birth control pills deductible?
KAY

DEAR KAY: Only if they don't work.

DEAR ABBY: I am eleven years old but I know all the facts of life because we live in a dirty neighborhood. My problem is that in my family we get pregnate quick. What I mean is, my sister got pregnate when she was fifteen just sitting next to a boy in church. That is what they say anyway. Can this be true?
DONNA LEE

DEAR DONNA LEE: No, somebody must have moved.

DEAR ABBY: Our son was married in January. Five months

later his wife had a ten-pound baby girl. They said the baby was premature. Tell me, can a baby this big be that early?

WONDERING

DEAR WONDERING: The baby was on time, the wedding was late. Forget it.

DEAR ABBY: Do you think about dying much?

CURIOUS

DEAR CURIOUS: No, it's the last thing I want to do.

DEAR ABBY: Is it possible for a man to be in love with two women at the same time?

JAKE

DEAR JAKE: Yes, and also hazardous.

DEAR ABBY: I know boys will be boys, but my "boy" is seventy-three and he's still chasing women. Any suggestions?

ANNIE

DEAR ANNIE: Don't worry. My dog has been chasing cars for years, but if he ever caught one, he wouldn't know what to do with it.

DEAR ABBY: I hope you won't think this is too dumb to

answer. Can a girl get pregnant from kissing with her mouth open?

CINDY

DEAR CINDY: No, but it's a good beginning.

DEAR ABBY: My husband, being a minister, has very little time for marriage relations, so he sets aside one night a week, which is Sunday, then he goes at it for all he is worth. On Monday morning I am dead tired and can't do the washing. What should I do?

RUBY IN ASHVILLE

DEAR RUBY: Wash on Tuesdays.

— ♥ —

Puns are fun and even though they more often than not elicit groans, I'm not above punning when the occasion presents itself:

DEAR ABBY: My husband and I have been invited to spend our vacation with friends who live in another state. They are a nice couple and we like them a lot, but here's the problem.

The last time we visited them the bedbugs almost ate us up alive. We never mentioned it, so don't know if the situation has changed or not. They want us again this year. Should we take a chance and go?

R AND G

DEAR R AND G: Only if you're really itching to see them.

DEAR ABBY: The woman who "talked to her plants" is not ready for the booby hatch. Plants not only respond to the right language, they are affected by music. For years the Carnation milk people have had piped music in their barns to keep their cows contented.

CLARA IN PHOENIX

DEAR CLARA: Are you pulling my leg, or udder-wise?

DEAR ABBY: Do you think that girls with glasses are as attractive as girls without them?

NANCY

DEAR NANCY: It depends on their frames.

DEAR ABBY: I am an eighteen-year-old girl, and my mother doesn't like some of the boys I go around with because they have beards. They aren't big, shaggy, dirty-looking beards— but small, neatly trimmed, clean-looking beards and I think they look sharp.

My mother says they look like a bunch of bums who will never amount to anything.

How can I convince her she is wrong?

LIKES BEARDS

DEAR LIKES: Remind her of the Smith Brothers. They coughed up a fortune.

DEAR ABBY: Are there any methods of birth control that are

positively foolproof?

                                                MIMI

DEAR MIMI: Sulfa denial and no acetol.

DEAR ABBY: To bra or not to bra? That's the question. Large, medium, small, or nonexistent; what's all the fuss about?

                                                NEIL

DEAR NEIL: As any geometry student knows, curves are nothing more than wrecked-angles.

DEAR ABBY: Last year while my husband was going with another woman he gave her a watch for Christmas. They had a fight in February and he broke up with her and asked for the watch. She gave it to him. Now my husband says I can have the watch if I want it. It looks as good as new. Should I wear it?

                                                NOT PROUD

DEAR NOT: Why not—if it keeps time. (Look inside. Maybe he gave the other woman "the works.")

DEAR ABBY: What do you think of a thirty-five-year-old married woman who wasn't satisfied with her 34B bust, had silicone implants, and now she's a 40D?

                                                JUST ASKING

DEAR JUST: It's all right with me. Maybe she wants the "booby" prize.

Had enough one-liners? If not, here is a potpourri. Help yourself:

DEAR ABBY: I have always wanted to have my family history traced, but I can't afford to spend a lot of money to do it. Any suggestions?

SAM IN CAL.

DEAR SAM: Yes. Run for public office.

DEAR ABBY: What inspires you most to write?

TED

DEAR TED: The Bureau of Internal Revenue.

DEAR ABBY: Is it possible for a woman to conceive under water? I mean in a pool, river, or bath.

MUST KNOW

DEAR MUST: Not without a man.

DEAR ABBY: I'm crazy about this guy, but he had some bad experiences with girls and I can't get anyplace with him. How can I prove to him that all girls aren't alike?

SHELLY

DEAR SHELLY: Take him to the beach!

DEAR ABBY: Can you please tell me where the custom of kissing a lady's hand originated? And why?

CHARLES

DEAR CHARLES: It originated in France, and since a person has to start somewhere, that's as good a place as any.

DEAR ABBY: Do you think a girl should keep a kosher kitchen for her husband?

FLORENCE

DEAR FLORENCE: Only if he's Jewish.

DEAR ABBY: I saw a man on the commuter train reading a book titled *Dear Abby* and he sure seemed to be enjoying it. I suppose you wrote it. Please send me the book and if it's any good I'll send you a check.

RUSSELL

DEAR RUSSELL: Send me the check and if it's any good I'll send you the book.

DEAR ABBY: On which side does a woman wear a flower in her hair if she wants to let men know she's available? I'm going to Hawaii soon and must know.

CANDY

DEAR CANDY: A flower over the left ear means I'm taken, a flower over the right ear means I'm available, and a flower over both ears means let's negotiate.

DEAR ABBY: Two men just bought an old mansion across the street and fixed it up. We notice a very suspicious mixture of people coming and going at all hours. Blacks, whites, orientals, women who look like men and men who look like women. We even saw a nun and a priest go inside. People come in everything from motorcycles to Cadillacs. This has always been considered one of the finest sections of San Francisco and these weirdos are giving it a bad name. How can we improve the neighborhood?

NOB HILL RESIDENTS

DEAR RESIDENTS: You could move.

DEAR ABBY: What's so special about a heterosexual relationship?

GAY AND HAPPY

DEAR GAY: You're not apt to get your socks mixed up.

DEAR ABBY: When you are being introduced, is it all right to say, "I've heard a lot about you"?

RITA

DEAR RITA: It depends on what you've heard.

DEAR ABBY: Why would a man check up on his wife to be sure he knows where she is every minute? Do you think he suspects that she's playing around?

SUE

DEAR SUE: Maybe he wants to know where she is while he's playing around.

DEAR ABBY: My husband is a traveling salesman, but I never worry about him cheating on me when he's on the road. I solved that problem years ago. Know how?

I tire him out so good when he's home, he's lucky if he has enough energy to carry his sample cases to the car.

SECURE IN SYRACUSE

DEAR SECURE: I don't want to worry you, lady, but a man can have the finest banquet in the world and six hours later he's hungry again!

DEAR ABBY: I am forty-four years old and I would like to meet a man my age with no bad habits.

ROSE

DEAR ROSE: So would I.

DEAR ABBY: What's the difference between a wife and a mistress?

BESS

DEAR BESS: Night and day.

DEAR ABBY: I've been sleeping with a piece of wedding cake

under my pillow every night since June 17 because I heard it would get me a man. Is this true?

ALWAYS A BRIDESMAID

DEAR ALWAYS: I can't guarantee you a man, but you'll get plenty of ants.

DEAR ABBY: What factor do you think is the most essential if a woman is to have a lasting marriage?

DOTTY

DEAR DOTTY: A lasting husband.

DEAR ABBY: Would you please tell me the difference between a maid and a housewife?

HOUSEWIFE

DEAR HOUSEWIFE: If you have a maid, you better keep your eye on your husband.

DEAR ABBY: If you were elected president, what's the first thing you'd do.

FRED

DEAR FRED: I'd ask for a recount.

'Encore, Encore!!'

Over the years readers have written to request that I rerun a certain column or letter. Many tell me that they have carried a favorite clipping around for so long it has become dog-eared and too worn out to read.

While some encores add a touch of humor to a universal experience, others are a somber reminder of the consequences of thoughtless behavior.

Twenty years ago I printed a letter signed "Too Late," and judging from the number of requests I've had over the years to run it again, that letter obviously touched a sensitive nerve with a great number of "Dear Abby" readers. "Too Late's" poignant plea says something about the way some folks treat their aging parents—and what it says is not very pretty:

DEAR ABBY: I am the most heartbroken person on earth. I always found time to go everywhere else but to see my old, gray-haired parents. They sat at home, loving me just the same. It is too late now to give them those few hours of happiness I was too selfish and too busy to give, and now when I go visit their graves and look at the green grass above them, I wonder if God will ever forgive me for the heartaches I must have caused them. I pray that you will print this, Abby, to tell those who still have parents to visit them and show their love and respect while there is still time. For it is later than you think.

Too Late

Another favorite with readers is "A Mother-in-Law's Prayer." I'm told when this has been read at bridal showers it breaks the ice and puts everyone in a jovial mood. It's all in fun, of course, except if the bride is really pregnant or the parents of the bride and the parents of the groom get along like the legendary Montagues and Capulets:

A Mother-in-Law's Prayer

O, Lord, help me to be glad when my son (or daughter) picks a mate. If he brings home a girl with two heads, help me to love both of them equally. And when my son says: "Mom, I want to get married," forbid that I should blurt out: "How far along is she?"

And please, Lord, help me to get through the wedding preparations without a squabble with the "other side." And drive from my mind the belief that had my child waited awhile, he or she could have done better.

Dear Lord, remind me daily that when I become a grandmother, my children don't want any advice on how to raise their children any more than I did when I was raising mine.

If you will help me to do these things, perhaps my children will find me a joy to be around, and maybe I won't have to write a "Dear Abby" letter complaining about my children neglecting me.

A class of sixth graders in a Milwaukee public school wrote to ask me for my definition of maturity. I hurriedly dashed off a succinct and oversimplified definition. It was published in their school newspaper and a copy was sent to me. It looked so good in print I decided to use it in my column. It has since been reprinted in many other publications, and I still get requests to run it again:

Maturity is the ability:
to do a job whether you're supervised or not;
to finish a job once it's started;
to carry money without spending it;
and to bear an injustice without wanting to get even.

"The Other Woman" has always been a hot topic. An extraordinary number of requests to run it again followed the appearance of this letter:

DEAR ABBY: May I give your readers the benefit of my very valuable experience? I address this to any woman who is in love with a married man:

Never expect to see him on Sundays or holidays. Never call him at home. Don't ever expect him to take you out in public, but be prepared to entertain him at your place. He may bring a bottle or the steaks occasionally, but in actual dollars and cents, you will spend more on him that he'll ever spend on you.

Never depend on him in times of personal crisis. Don't believe him when he tells you that his wife is a shrew, cold, homely, too fat (or too thin), and she hasn't slept with him in ten years.

Don't expect his wife to divorce him if she catches him. She knows that you aren't his first and won't be his last. Also, she's not about to give up her social status, financial security, and retirement income because of you. However, her discovery will probably terminate his affair with you, so be prepared to get some new clothes, circulate, and find another man whose wife is a shrew, cold, homely, too fat (or too thin), and hasn't slept with him for ten years. Sign me. . .

HIS WIFE

An unidentified reader sent me a chilling piece containing an important message titled, "Please, God, I'm Only Seventeen." Seldom have I been so moved by a letter. I shared it with my readers.

"PLEASE, GOD, I'M ONLY SEVENTEEN"

"The day I died was an ordinary school day. How I wish I had taken the bus! But I was too cool for the bus. I remember how I wheedled the car out of Mom. 'Special favor,' I pleaded. 'All the kids drive.' When the 2:50 bell rang, I threw all my books in the locker. I was free until 8:40 tomorrow morning! I ran to the parking lot . . . excited at the thought of driving a car and being my own boss. Free!

"It doesn't matter how the accident happened. I was goofing off . . . going too fast. Taking crazy chances. But I was enjoying my freedom and having fun. The last thing

I remember was passing an old lady who seemed to be going awfully slow. I heard the deafening crash and felt a terrific jolt. Glass and steel flew everywhere. My whole body seemed to be turning inside out. I heard myself scream.

"Suddenly I awakened. It was very quiet. A police officer was standing over me. Then I saw a doctor. My body was mangled, I was saturated with blood. Pieces of jagged glass were sticking out all over. Strange that I couldn't feel anything.

"Hey, don't pull that sheet over my head. I can't be dead. I'm only seventeen, I've got a date tonight. I am supposed to grow up and have a wonderful life. I haven't lived yet. I can't be dead.

"Later I was placed in a drawer. My folks had to identify me. Why did they have to see me like this? Why did I have to look at Mom's eyes when she faced the most terrible ordeal of her life? Dad suddenly looked like an old man. He told the man in charge, 'Yes, he is my son.'

"The funeral was a weird experience. I saw all my relatives and friends walk toward the casket. They passed by, one by one, and looked at me with the saddest eyes I've ever seen. Some of my buddies were crying. A few of the girls touched my hand and sobbed as they walked away.

"Please . . . somebody . . . wake me up! Get me out of here. I can't bear to see my Mom and Dad so broken up. My grandparents are so racked with grief they can barely walk. My brother and sisters are like zombies. They move like robots. In a daze, everybody! No one can believe this. And, I can't believe it either.

"Please don't bury me! I'm not dead! I have a lot of living to do! I want to laugh and run again. I want to sing and dance. Please don't put me in the ground. I promise if you give me just one more chance, God, I'll be the most careful driver in the whole world. All I want is one more chance. Please, God, I'm only seventeen!"

The need for attending church is sometimes questioned by the very young. Judging from the requests to print this letter again, it was very much appreciated by my reading audience:

DEAR ABBY: I am a thirteen-year-old boy, and my parents force me to go to church every Sunday.

I hate going to church because I see people there who I know are drunkards, gossips, liars, and cheats, and they are right there every Sunday saying their prayers and singing hymns. I don't have any respect for hypocrites, and our church is full of them, my own parents included.

I am only thirteen, so maybe my opinion doesn't count, but I don't see any sense in my going to church with a bunch of hypocrites.

ONLY A BOY

DEAR ONLY: Christ became a man at thirteen, and you are not too young to become a man either. One goes to church to learn about the Bible and the word of the Lord, although God dwells in one's heart, and it's not necessary to "go" to church to communicate with Him. And as for the "hypocrites" you see in church—what better place is there for them to be?

A church is not a museum for saints. It's a hospital for sinners.

Even grownups who see the value of church don't necessarily agree with the price. I received over three hundred requests to print this item in various church bulletins. And

Lord only knows how many have printed it without my permission:

> DEAR ABBY: We are not overly religious people, but we do like to go to church once in a while. It seems to me that every time we turn around in church, we are getting hit for money. I thought religion was free. I realize that churches need some money but I think it is getting to be a racket. Just what do churches do with all their money?
>
> CURIOUS

> DEAR CURIOUS: Even priests, ministers and rabbis must eat. And since they work full time at their tasks, the churches must support them. Staff, professional choir members, and musicians also must be paid. Buildings must be maintained, heated, lighted, and beautified. (And of course, first they must be built!)
>
> Custodial staff must eat and feed their families. Most churches engage in philanthropic work (aid to needy, missions, and education); hence, they have their financial obligations. Even orchids, contrary to folklore, do not live on air. Churches can't live on air, either.
>
> Religion, like water, may be free, but when they pipe it to you, you've got to help pay for the piping. And the piper!

Then I committed the ultimate chutzpah. I actually sat down and wrote Ten Commandments for Wives:

TEN COMMANDMENTS FOR WIVES

1. Defile not thy body either with excessive foods, tobacco or alcohol, that thy days may be long in the house which thy husband provideth for thee.

2. Put thy husband before thy mother, thy father, thy daughter, and thy son, for he is thy lifelong companion.

3. Thou shalt not nag.

4. Permit no one to tell thee that thou art having a hard time of it; neither thy mother, thy sister, nor thy neighbors, for the Judge will not hold her guiltless who letteth another disparage her husband.

5. Thou shalt not withhold affection from thy husband, for every man loveth to be loved.

6. Forget not the virtue of cleanliness and modest attire.

7. Forgive with grace, for who among us doth not need forgiveness?

8. Remember that the frank approval of thy husband is worth more to thee than the admiring glances of a hundred strangers.

9. Keep thy home in good order, for out of it come the joys of thy old age.

10. Honor the Lord thy God all the days of thy life, and thy children will raise up and call thee blessed.

After that hit print I was forced by popular demand to compose Ten Commandments for Husbands:

TEN COMMANDMENTS FOR HUSBANDS

1. Thou shalt put thy wife before thy mother, thy father, thy daughter, and thy son, for she is thy lifelong companion.

2. Abuse not thy body either with excessive food, tobacco, or drink, that thy days may be many and healthful in the presence of thy loved ones.

3. Permit neither thy business nor thy hobby to make of thee a stranger to thy children, for the precious gift a man giveth his family is his time.

4. Forget not the virtue of cleanliness.

5. Make not thy wife a begger, but share willingly with her thy worldly goods.

6. Forget not to say, "I love you," for even though thy love be constant, thy wife doth yearn to hear the words.

7. Remember that the approval of thy wife is worth more than the admiring glances of a hundred strangers. Cleave unto her and forsake all others.

8. Keep thy home in good repair, for out of it come the joys of thy old age.

9. Forgive with grace. For who among us doth not need to be forgiven?

10. Honor the Lord thy God all the days of thy life, and thy children will rise up and call thee blessed.

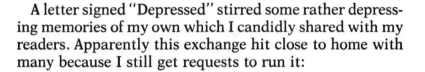

A letter signed "Depressed" stirred some rather depressing memories of my own which I candidly shared with my readers. Apparently this exchange hit close to home with many because I still get requests to run it:

DEAR ABBY: About a month ago we had a flash flood, and I lost nearly all the treasures I had saved for forty-five years. Albums filled with pictures and snapshots, letters, clippings—none of which can be replaced. I had them stored in plastic containers, and when I opened them, all I found was mud and water!

It seems that a part of my life is gone, and I am heartsick over it. I am sixty and have had a very happy life. Our children are married and gone, and there are just the two of us.

I've tried to keep busy and not dwell on my loss, but it is on my mind constantly. I wish I could forget this terrible nightmare.

Somehow I feel that you can help me. Abby, have you ever lost any of your treasures? And if you have, how did you get over it?

DEPRESSED

DEAR DEPRESSED: Yes, Dear. I lost my beautiful mother in 1945. (She was only fifty-seven.) And a few years later, I lost a wonderful father. (He was sixty-two.) And not a day passes that I don't thank God for letting me have my parents for as long as I did. I know many who were not nearly as blessed as I, and I think of those who have survived a far greater tragedy—losing their children.

Now, what were you saying about clippings and pictures and other "treasures"?

Eight years ago I wrote a special column for Thanksgiving. One might say my readers gobbled it up. In any case it has been so well received it has become my annual column.

DEAR READERS: Today is Thanksgiving, so take a few minutes to think about what you have to be thankful for.

How's your health? Not so good? Well, thank God you've lived this long. A lot of people haven't. You're hurting? Thousands—maybe millions—are hurting more. (Have you ever visited a veterans' hospital? Or a rehabilitation clinic for crippled children?)

If you awakened this morning and were able to hear the birds sing, use your vocal chords to utter human sounds, walk to the breakfast table on two good legs, and read the newspaper with two good eyes—praise the Lord! A lot of people couldn't.

How's your pocketbook? Thin? Well, most of the living

world is a lot poorer. No pensions. No welfare. No food stamps. No Social Security. In fact, one-third of the people in the world will go to bed hungry tonight.

Are you lonely? The way to have a friend is to be one. If nobody calls you, call them. Go out of your way to do something nice for somebody. It's a sure cure for the blues.

Are you concerned about your country's future? Hooray! Our system has been saved by such concern. Concern for honesty in government, concern for peace, and concern for fair play under the law. Your country may not be a rose garden, but it also is not a patch of weeds.

Freedom rings! Look and listen. You can still worship at the church of your choice, cast a secret ballot, and even criticize your government without fearing a knock on the head or a knock at the door at midnight. And if you want to live under a different system, you are free to go. There are no walls or fences—nothing to keep you here.

As a final thought, I'll repeat my Thanksgiving Prayer:
O, heavenly Father: We thank Thee for food and
   remember the hungry
We thank Thee for health and remember the sick
We thank Thee for friends and remember the
   friendless
We thank Thee for freedom and remember the
   enslaved,
May these remembrances stir us to service
That Thy gifts to us may be used for others.
Amen.

Have a wonderful Thanksgiving and may God bless you and yours.

LOVE,
ABBY

I don't know how you feel about the annual Christmas

newsletter but I think it's a neat way for busy people to keep in touch with friends and relatives. However, a reader named Elaine wrote to express an opposing view:

DEAR ABBY: Please lambast the utter conceit of people who send mimeographed "newsletters" to friends as a special "Christmas treat." They all sound like this:

"Dear friends, George is now chairman of the board, having passed the presidency of his company on to Melvin, our new son-in-law, who won the club golf championship last year. Mel was so proud of our Peg when she was elected treasurer of the Junior League that he surprised her with a new Mercedes. Our little beauty, Judy, was runner-up for Homecoming Queen and also made National Honor Society. Timmy was accepted at Yale, Harvard, Dartmouth, and Princeton, but he thinks he'll go to a little junior college upstate. I took the part of the mother in "The Graduate" for our Annual Hospital Charity show. We got a director in from New York and he said I was as good as Ann Bancroft."

Blah, blah, blah, nothing but brag, brag, brag. It's nauseating!

Next year, Bob and I are going to send these bores our own Christmas letter, and it will go like this:

"Hi, Everybody. Well, another year has passed. Grandpa fell down the cellar steps and broke his hip. (Good thing we kept Bob's crutches after his ski accident.) Our eldest doll Susie is having her problems. Her fiance called off the engagement and we don't know what to tell people. My sister's daughter didn't go back to school this quarter. They claim it's mononucleosis, but she has suddenly put on a lot of weight, and looks slightly p.g. to me. With everything so high these days, looks like Bob will have to borrow on his life insurance again to pay his taxes. Well, things could be worse. If his mother sells her house and moves in with us, I'll kill myself. Gotta run. The whole family is down

with flu, and guess who the nurse is? Merry Christmas!"
ELAINE

A few years ago I thought it would be appropriate to publish some resolutions on New Year's Day. As I began to write them I recalled something in the Overeaters Anonymous literature that said in essence what I had in mind. I found it, made some revisions and came up with a column that has become a New Year's Day tradition.

1. Just for today I will try to live through this day only, and not set far-reaching goals to try to overcome all my problems at once. I know I can do something for twelve hours that would appall me if I felt that I had to keep it up for a lifetime.

2. Just for today I will try to be happy. Abraham Lincoln said, "Most folks are about as happy as they make up their minds to be." He was right. I will not dwell on thoughts that depress me. I will chase them out of my mind and replace them with happy thoughts.

3. Just for today I will adjust myself to what is. I will face reality. I will try to change those things which I can change, and accept those things I cannot change.

4. Just for today I will try to improve my mind. I will not be a mental loafer. I will force myself to read something that requires effort, thought, and concentration.

5. Just for today I will exercise my soul in three ways: I will do a good deed for somebody—without letting them know it. (If they find out I did it, it won't count.) I will do at least two things that I know I should do but have been putting off. I will not show anyone that my feelings are hurt; they may be hurt, but today I will not show it.

6. Just for today I will be agreeable. I will look as well

as I can, dress becomingly, talk softly, act courteously, and speak ill of no one. Just for today I'll not try to improve anybody except myself.

7. Just for today I will have a program. I may not follow it exactly, but I will have it, thereby saving myself from two pests: hurry and indecision.

8. Just for today I will have a quiet half hour to relax alone. During this time I will reflect on my behavior and will try to get a better perspective on my life.

9. Just for today I will be unafraid. I will gather the courage to do what is right and take the responsibility for my own actions. I will expect nothing from the world, but I will realize that as I give to the world, the world will give to me.

— ♥ —

On my twenty-fifth wedding anniversary, I ran the following letter to my husband. Others who wanted to express appreciation to their husbands on their anniversaries have asked me to repeat it. I was happy to oblige because the words are as true today as they were seventeen years ago.

DEAR MORT:
July 2, 1964
Today is a very special day for me. It's my twenty-fifth wedding anniversary, and I have this to say: I had a mother and father who really loved each other, so I know what love is.

I have worked hard to see two teen-agers safely through their traumatic teens, so I know what satisfaction is.

I have prayed. And my prayers have been answered, so I know what faith is.

I have had by my side the kindest, gentlest, most considerate human being I've ever known, so I know what happiness is.

And because I've known all these things . . . I know what wealth is.

I love you.

ABBY

Not Fit To Print

I have a fascinating collection in my files not fit to print. Some I've tidied up for publication, others remain intact. After long deliberation I have decided to share some printable material from my "Not Fit to Print" files:

DEAR ABBY: We work in a large office. Our office manager, I'll call him Marvin, is a middle-aged family man. The boss's secretary, I'll call her Sissy, is a shapely young divorcee. Since Sissy came to work here, she and Marvin have been spending a lot of time together in the file room with the door locked. What they do in there is their business, but we're tired of covering up for them when the boss comes looking for Sissy. What do you suggest?

THE OFFICE GANG

DEAR GANG: Next time the boss comes looking for Sissy, tell him to look in the file room under "Marvin."

— ♥ —

DEAR ABBY: Awhile back you did a whole column on what men notice first about a woman. Some men say they notice her face, her legs, her behind, but most men said they notice the size of her boobs. Well the first thing I notice about a woman is the size of her *husband*.

FREDDIE

DEAR ABBY: My husband falls into bed dead tired every night. He never gives me as much as a good-night peck on the cheek. Then about four o'clock in the morning he wakes up full of pep and feeling amorous and he forces his affection on me without saying a word. Then he rolls over and goes to sleep. All the while I'm laying there like a statue. Could you call this statutory rape?

DEAR ABBY: I went with this guy for three years. He was the first guy I ever dated. All in all, I loaned him $300. I know there isn't anything I can do about my virginity, but what are my chances for getting my money back?

DEAR ABBY: I've been married for six years and have five kids. No twins. My husband still wants sex every night and sometimes in the morning too. I told him he should get himself a hobby, and he says that *is* his hobby.

DEAR MISS VAN BUREN: Can you please give me all the information you have on the rhythm system? I'm learning how to dance.

Of course most people don't realize how funny they are. Some excerpts.

. . . I didn't know what got into my seventy-two-year-old husband until the doctor explained it to me. He said that some older men get an irritation in their urinal tract and they mistake it for passion.

. . . I'm old enough to take precautions but I'm not old enough to buy any.

. . . My analyst asked me to tell him about my very first satisfying sexual experience. Of course I was alone at the time.

. . . About the only time he has anything to do with me is when I'm asleep. I wouldn't say he is kinky exactly, but he says he really gets turned on when I pretend I'm dead.

. . . I'm fifteen and I think I'm pregnant and if I am, I don't know who the baby's daddy is because my mother would never let me go steady.

... I have a man I never could trust. Why, he cheats so much I'm not even sure this baby I'm carrying is his.

... Abby, what do you think of married women who wear shorts in the business section?

... Can a person get poison oak through clothes? My boyfriend got the most terrible case you ever saw. I don't even want to tell you where he got it the worst. Answer right away because if he couldn't possibly have gotten it through his pants, we are through.

... I am a twenty-three-year-old liberated woman who has been on the pill for two years. It's getting pretty expensive and I think my boyfriend should share half the cost, but I don't know him well enough to discuss money with him.

... I just heard of some kind of powder medicine called "Soft Peter." It's supposed to quiet down a man's desire. Please tell me where I can buy some, as I'd like to give it to my husband on weekends.

... It says in the Bible, "Love One Another." Well, I don't go that far, but I do try to wear a smile in public.

... I asked my husband if he ever heard of foreplay. And he thought I wanted to invite another couple over and switch partners.

... I told my doctor that my husband cried like a baby when I refused to have sex with him and the doctor asked me what my husband's IQ was. Abby, what's an IQ?

... Then you told some woman whose husband had lost all interest in sex to send him to a doctor. Well, my husband lost all interest in sex years ago and he is a doctor.

... I am nine and live on a farm. My sister is fifteen and pregnant. I never knew you could get this kind of service without a husband.

... Good God! You never heard such talk from a lady. The worst four-letter word she called him had a lot more than four letters in it.

... He came right out and admitted that he was a sexagenerian. Well I suppose it's his business, but do you think he should have said that in mixed company?

... This is the second marriage for both of us. And when my husband said "I Will" he knew damn well he couldn't.

... I've been doing a lot of reading lately and I have just discovered that my husband is no bargain. Anyway, everytime I catch my husband with another woman he buys me something real nice. I now have a fur coat, a color TV, a new washer/dryer, and a double-door refrigerator.

. . . I'm a good Christian woman who loves her husband, but he wants me to use really vulgar words when we are making love. I only know three. Could you suggest any new ones?

. . . Abby, thanks for nothing. Your suggestion that I report that guy in my platoon to my sergeant is useless. My sergeant is one of the guys he's going with.

. . . I asked him if he had had a vasectomy and he said yes. Well later he told me he thought that meant did he ever have his tonsils out.

. . . I just found out I'm pregnant. Will you please send me a booklet on how to have a lovely wedding?

Every now and then a typographical error occurs which makes for hilarious reading. This appeared in the *International Herald Tribune* in Hamburg, Germany, under a column titled, "People":

The heartwarming story of the month, meanwhile, is submitted by E. F. Clark, from the pages of the *Rome Daily American*: "In a plea for advice from columnist Abigail Van Buren, a sweet little old lady faithful and understanding beyond the pale writes, 'Dear Abby: I am seventy-five years old. My husband recently assed away. And according to his wishes I had his remains remated.'"

— ♥ —

Some other typos forwarded to me by my readers:

It was not love at all but only a passing fanny.

I put a lock on my door and now he has to rape to get in.

I hate three children by my first marriage.

I am divorced and getting married soon but I haven't selected a mate yet.

Where should I go to get my face listed?

Please tell your readers to think twice before marrying a window.

Can you recommend an inexpensive place for unfed mothers?

He invited me to an informal fathering.

I didn't say anything because I didn't want to get my sister in bed with her boss.

They travel together because that's the way they make the best loving.

I later learned that my husband tried to make it with our 115-year-old babysitter.

I went to court and was represented by a woman who was a great layer.

— ♥ —

Where the typo occurs, some editors apologize and print corrections. I offer the following example of a typographical error that appeared in the classified section of a small California newspaper. They should have left bad enough alone, as is evident by the subsequent disastrous attempts to correct it.

MONDAY:—For Sale: R. D. Jones has one sewing machine for sale. Phone 948-0707 after 7 p.m. and ask for Mrs. Kelly who lives with him cheap.

TUESDAY:—Notice: We regret having erred in R. D. Jones' ad yesterday. It should have read, "One sewing machine for sale cheap. Phone 948-0707 and ask for Mrs. Kelly who lives with him after 7 p.m."

WEDNESDAY:—Notice: R. D. Jones has informed us that he has received several annoying telephone calls because of the error we made in his classified ad yesterday. The ad stands correct as follows:
"For Sale—R. D. Jones has one sewing machine for sale.

Cheap. Phone 948-0707 after 7 p.m. and ask for Mrs. Kelly who loves with him."

THURSDAY:—Notice: I, R. D. Jones, have no sewing machine for sale. I smashed it. Don't call 948-0707 as the telephone has been out. I have not been carrying on with Mrs. Kelly. Until yesterday she was my housekeeper but she quit.

A few years ago I received a letter from a middle-aged unmarried woman who had sought psychiatric help to relieve her feelings of inadequacy, loneliness, and depression. She said her psychiatrist, whom I shall call "Dr. Strangelove," because I don't want to be sued, was the "fatherly" type. He told her that she needed to feel wanted and loved, so in addition to her regular weekly visits, he provided the "love" she needed on his couch—on weekends.

The lady's complaint was that her doctor had been billing her for the weekend sessions, which annoyed her because he seemed to be getting as much out of them as she.

I immediately sent her letter to Dr. Judd Marmor, my friend and valued psychiatric consultant, and asked him to please check out Dr. Strangelove's credentials. Much to my amazement, I learned that Dr. Strangelove was a member of the American Psychiatric Association!

I advised the woman to report her doctor to the Ethics Committee of the American Psychiatric Association.

It seems that Dr. Strangelove, who was over seventy at the time, had just published a paper in an obscure sex research journal stating that in his forty years of practice he had treated over eight hundred females and, as part of the "treatment," he'd had sexual intercourse with over four hundred of them!

In winding up the correspondence with Dr. Marmor, I jokingly wrote:

I think a fitting epitaph for this psychiatrist would be:
"Here lies Dr. Strangelove
Who claimed much progress made
He said he laid four hundred patients
I think he lied more than he laid."

All Kidding Aside

I'm asked almost daily, "What kind of moron writes to a newspaper columnist for advice?"

I've said repeatedly that the person who is smart enough to know that he has a problem—and wants *to do* something about it—is no moron.

Then there are those who ask, "Why do *you* think people write to you?" Since the people who write to me represent the broadest cross-section of men, women, and children imaginable, they write for a variety of reasons.

Many hope to find quick and easy solutions to complex problems they've struggled with for years. Others don't really want an answer, they just want to tell somebody their side of it without being interrupted or questioned. Some are too ashamed of their problem to face their own clergyman, and many don't belong to a church. Others write to complain, unload, confess, or sound off. Some are just plain lonely and have no one to talk to. They trust me. And the price is right.

Of course, I get my share of kooks and "creative" writers who fabricate problems just to see if they can get them published, but I can usually spot the phonies.

But most people who write to Dear Abby are not aware of the help available to them in their own communities. (I keep up-to-date files of all the "help" agencies in every community that runs my column.)

My column is only a tip of a very large iceberg. At the bottom of each column is (or should be) the tag, "For a personal reply, write to Dear Abby in care of your newspaper. And please enclose a stamped, self-addressed envelope."

All who request personal unpublished replies receive them. I don't use form letters.

I've never had a press agent, I have no ghost writers. Every column, book, and article that bears my name is written by yours truly. If some of the signatures sound contrived, it's because the writer has either provided a fictitious name or has asked me to do so.

Although I have a staff of competent, caring assistants, all personally trained by me, I still answer many of the unpublished letters myself. I also telephone those whose problems are urgent—a despondent reader who threatens suicide or a friendless girl frantically searching for a safe, legal abortion or a home for unwed mothers.

When I tell them it's "Dear Abby" calling, at first they think someone is putting them on. They can't believe that I would care enough to phone personally.

I'm asked, "To what do you attribute the success of your column?"

It's brief, to the point, and written in language that everybody can understand. I also select letters that I think will appeal to a wide variety of readers: the young, middle-aged, elderly, the sophisticates, squares, gays, straights, kooks, and conservatives.

Occasionally I publish letters from people who want only to air their pet peeves or to state their views. Almost every letter begets another letter, and another and another, until I have to end the debate lest my readers write the entire column.

I'm sure that some read "Dear Abby" for entertainment. Others are looking for answers to their problems. Many are fascinated with keyhole peeking—getting their kicks from reading about the intimacies of someone else's private life.

I know that many read my column for comfort. It's reassuring to know that others suffer from the same feeling of anger, jealousy, hostility, insecurity, and guilt that plague them. Misery does loves company.

I've published letters on every conceivable subject, from shoplifting to face-lifting. In one week, I've dealt with mastectomies, vasectomies, bed-wetting, child-molesting, acne, arson, incest, rape, and false fannies.

I regard my column as a subtle educational device.

I've visited mental institutions, nursing homes, penal institutions, and animal shelters. I've also attended meetings of Alcoholics Anonymous, Gamblers Anonymous, and Overeaters Anonymous.

Having strong feelings about one's right to die with dignity, I publicly endorsed the Living Will—a document instructing my family, my physicians, my clergyman, etc., that "should I become terminally ill, I do not want to have my life prolonged by artificial measures."

I'm told that due to the publicity I gave it in my column, I was largely responsible for placing no less than four million Living Wills into the hands of those who shared my views.

My concern about the threat of overpopulation, plus the importance of educating the world about birth control and venereal disease made of me a True Believer in and staunch supporter of Planned Parenthood.

And to quote Freud, "Since nothing that is human is

alien to me," in an effort to learn more about the trans-sexual phenomenon, I attended an international weekend seminar at Stanford University. There I met transsexuals, some of whom had already had sex reassignment surgery and others still anticipating it.

Gathered there were some of the world's most knowl-edgeable psychiatrists, endocrinologists, and surgeons—courageous pioneers who had come to share their knowl-edge about transsexualism, a human condition that is still tragically buried in ignorance.

My twenty-five years as Dear Abby have been fulfilling, exciting, and incredibly rewarding. My career has brought me awards, citations, and honors far beyond what I de-served. I've lost track of the number of babies who were named after me. Not to mention the horses, dogs, cats, mice, and a chimpanzee, too.

With the years I've become less flip and more aware of the enormous responsibility I have to my reading public.

I have had my finger on the pulse of the nation for two and a half decades, and I've concluded that people are better than ever.

With all the crime, violence, and rebellion that has sur-faced, I've seen more compassion, real love, and caring among the younger generation than was evidenced twenty-five years ago.

My readers have told me that they've learned from me. But it's the other way around. I've learned from *them*.

Has it been a lot of work? Not really. It's only work if you'd rather be doing something else.

DEAR ABBY: Between you and me, I think the people who write to you are either morons or they're just plain stupid.
                                        HENRY

DEAR HENRY: Which are you?